In this biography of Lady Caroline Lamb, Elizabeth Jenkins
has produced a sensitive and colourful portrait of Lady Caroline
and of the Regency era. Miss Jenkins has written many novels,
and her studies of *Elizabeth the Great, Jane Austen* and *Lady Caroline
Lamb* have been recognised as classics in the art of biography.

Also by Elizabeth Jenkins and available in Cardinal

JANE AUSTEN

Lady Caroline Lamb

Elizabeth Jenkins

CARDINAL edition published in 1974
by Sphere Books Ltd, 30/32 Gray's Inn Road,
London WC1X 8JL

First published in Great Britain by
Victor Gollancz Ltd 1932
Copyright © Elizabeth Jenkins 1932, 1972
Sphere Books revised edition 1972

Printed in Great Britain by
Hazell Watson & Viney Ltd,
Aylesbury, Bucks

ISBN 0 351 16937 7

To my Mother

My thanks are due to the following for their permission:

Lord Bessborough to quote from "The Private Correspondence of Earl Gower."

The Hon. Mrs. Hugh Wyndham, from "The Correspondence of Sarah, Lady Lyttelton."

Sir John Ponsonby, from "The Ponsonby Family."

Messrs. John Murray, from "The Correspondence of Lord Byron, chiefly with Lady Melbourne."

Messrs. Longmans, Green & Co., from "The Letters of Harriet, Countess of Granville."

Messrs. Blackie & Sons, from "The Two Duchesses," by Vere Foster.

DEVONSHIRE HOUSE

> *The Dome where pleasure holds her midnight reign,*
> *Here, richly decked, admits the gorgeous train:*
> *Tumultuous grandeur crowds the blazing square,*
> *The rattling chariots clash, the torches glare.*
>
> GOLDSMITH, 1769.

CHAPTER ONE

How beautiful London was in the last decades of the eighteenth and the first few decades of the nineteenth centuries can be dimly understood from prints, and from the actual relics of that time. The eye fastens upon these, striving at the same time to shut out the hideous wilderness which succeeding years have piled around them; one can still distinguish the two styles of eighteenth-century domestic architecture; the simpler, with its solid yet airy grace, its plain façades, its Grecian porticoes, and its fanlights; and the more splendid Palladian erections, with their fluted pillars and marble cornices. But it requires a strong effort of the imagination to see, as the Londoner of 1800 would have seen, these houses standing forth in their original freshness, clear of the encroachments of sham Gothic and modern concrete; with their white and yellow plaster and pale stonework uncontaminated in the smokeless air, while the architectural triumphs of the most civilised era the world has seen were enhanced by a rural loveliness almost unspoiled from the sixteenth century.

The combination of the charm of the country and the magnificence of town was perfectly shown in Piccadilly, where, opposite the green felicity of Green Park, stood Devonshire House, occupying, with its great forecourt and wrought-iron gates, the whole space between Berkeley Street and Stratton Street. This house, a true successor in size, splendour, and importance to the palaces of the Tudor nobles, was the very temple of Society, frequented by a "gorgeous train" headed by the Prince Regent, Fox and Sheridan. The brilliant epoch of its career began in 1775, when William Cavendish, fifth Duke of Devonshire, married Lady Georgiana Spencer, who, usually mentioned as "the beautiful Duchess," was considered to be the most fascinating woman of the age.

She and her sister Henrietta, the mother of Lady Caroline Lamb, were the daughters of John, first Earl Spencer, and his capable but unprepossessing wife, Miss Poyntz. Her grandson, Earl Cowper, said of the latter: "She was a woman who did not naturally possess any quickness of understanding, nor do I think she possessed any sterling good sense; but she had taken great pains with herself, had read a great deal and, though herself far from brilliant in conversation, had lived in the society of clever people. This gave her a reputation for ability to which she was not entitled." The daughters appear to have been as much unlike the mother as possible, unless it were in a deficiency, on the Duchess's part at least, of sterling good sense; the natural gifts of beauty, spirit, and charm with which they were so lavishly endowed, and the spontaneous, easy extravagance of their mode of existence, do not suggest in the slightest the mother who had had to take great pains with herself. The Duchess of Devonshire is described as having red-gold curling hair, grey eyes, and an always laughing mouth. Henrietta, Lady Bessborough, had dark eyes and hair, and a softer, less lively disposition, and was altogether perhaps the more interesting character of the two: but as Lady Caroline was for several years in the care—if care be the word—of the Duchess, and as her career shows so markedly the Duchess's influence, for the purposes of the former's biography the character of the aunt is as important as—perhaps even more important than—that of the mother.

Georgiana Spencer married at seventeen; a pamphleteer, remonstrating with her on the indecorum of her conduct, says that till her marriage, her education had been the object of unremitting attention from her excellent parents. Her niece, however, supplies a much more lively, and, one cannot but feel, in the light of the Duchess's career, a more convincing account: "Her marriage was one *de convenance*: her delight was hunting butterflies. The housekeeper's breaking a lathe over her head reconciled her to marriage. She was ignorant of everything." Ignorant, wild and loving, and astonishingly beautiful, she might have expected to have an eventful married life, even with a husband of influence and tact; the Duke of Devonshire, however, who once reproved her for sitting on his knee when her mother and sister were present, can have provided little outlet for the overflowing enthusiasm of her nature. She was perhaps driven to forming strong attachments outside her own family, although she and her sister remained devoted to each other; but beside her celebrated and enduring liaison with Fox, and her intimacy with the Prince Regent, her most ardent friendship was with Lady Elizabeth Foster, daughter of the Earl of Bristol, a sportsman and connoisseur with an Irish bishopric. Lady Elizabeth had the distinction of having refused a proposal from Gibbon while in Switzerland, and Gibbon's pronouncement on the two ladies was that "Bess is much nearer the level of a mortal, but a mortal for whom the wisest man, historic or medical, would throw away two or three worlds if he had them in his possession." She had a son, Augustus, by a husband who had divorced her, and she and Augustus Foster were intimately connected with Devonshire House; the friend of the Duchess and the mistress of the Duke, to the satisfaction of all three, on the former's death in 1806, she became the second Duchess of Devonshire.

To the man in the street, it is a vague idea of fantastic elegance rather than its homely vigour that "the eighteenth century" represents. The Duchess's early life was coincident with the era which seems most to account for this impression. At the period of her marriage, in 1775, the fashion in dress had reached its most exaggerated phase, the climax of extravagance before the reaction to the grace and simplicity of the "Empire" and "Regency" styles. The hair was powdered and trained over an erection of anything to two feet in height, to counterbalance which the skirt achieved an enormous circumference. The Duchess was among the first who added to the height of the coiffure by curling ostrich plumes. She appeared one night in her opera box, in answer to a squib of Sheridan's, shaded by a cloud of pink plumage, and under her ægis the fashion reached the point of absurdity. A print entitled "A Warning to Ladies to Take Care of Their Heads," published in 1778, shows a lady in full dress whose feathers have caught alight in the candles of the lofty chandelier. Her tastes and whims were so much in the public eye—in an era when Society consisted of three hundred persons, and the population of London itself numbered barely seven hundred thousand—that she was taken to represent in her own person the sins of society as a whole; a gentleman published in 1777 a letter of remonstrance addressed to her, in which he censures her especially for—"that preposterous plumage which was at once the ornament of your head and the emblem of yourself."

During the last fifteen years or so of the century, women's dress began to lose its sharp outline and to assume the looser, more natural lines which finally developed into the nymph-like fashions of the early nineteenth century. The Duchess of Devonshire is usually associated with the later fashions rather than the earlier; with the low-necked dress, with a fichu or frill round the shoulders, a sash tied round the waist, a long and flowing skirt, and one of those large, tilted hats to which she gave her name. She is said to have introduced the new fashion herself, and it must have suited her voluptuous attractions better than the rigidity of the former syle.

It was thus attired, no doubt, that in 1784 she and Lady Bessborough set out on the famous expedition to secure votes for Fox, and were described as "the prettiest pair of pictures that ever appeared on a *canvas*." The stories of this episode are classical; of how they entered taverns and shops in the lowest quarters of the town; any such radiant and fashionable ladies would have made a sensation in those surroundings, but the spirit of the Duchess turned the expedition into a triumph. She gave a butcher a kiss for the promise of his vote, while a labourer declared that her eyes were so bright he could light his pipe at them, and an Irish sweep said that if he were God, he would make her Queen of Heaven. This genius for getting on with people in any walk of life, which is a characteristic typical of the English aristocracy, is an indication of vitality and sincerity not associated with the ordinary fine lady. And, indeed, she had these qualities, obscured by others as they were; although Horace Walpole said, when her first child was born, "She will stuff the poor babe into her knotting bag when she wants to play *macao*," yet when she thought herself dying, she said good-bye to her son with the words, "Be brave, and always speak the truth."

Nevertheless, the usual tenor of her life appears to have been one of dissipation carried almost to the pitch of sublimity. It is curious, when studying the later life of Lady Bessborough, where she appears the complete picture of the tender, anxious mother, absorbed in her child, and suffering so much on her account that her constitution is quite broken down, to see her participating in all the frolics of the Duchess. She fully shared the latter's passion for gaming, which was devouring; Sheridan said that he once handed the Duchess into her carriage literally sobbing over her losses, and, although she once won £900 in a lottery, Walpole mentions that she and Lady Bessborough were indebted to the Jews for £23,000 for the discharge of gaming debts, while in 1797, Lady Bessborough was actually arrested and fined for gaming at the house of Lady Buckingham. One can imagine, however, that she was entirely swayed by her brilliant sister, as she was to be, to a certain degree, by her daughter. Her portraits show her as a most attractive creature, with her dark hair, large dark eyes, and a

12

bright yet tender expression. Her marriage with John Ponsonby, Viscount Duncannon, 3rd Earl of Bessborough, does not seem to have made, at first, any serious inroads on her leisure, any more than that of the Duchess occupied hers. The careers of the two sisters were outwardly not dissimilar—each had, among others, a liaison with a man of the first distinction, the Duchess's with Fox corresponding with Lady Bessborough's affair with Sheridan, a curious, perverted, and agonising struggle, from which she was too kind and too weak to break free, and which ended with Sheridan's last frightful message to her, that his eyes would be looking up through his coffin lid. Each had, of course, town and country houses; the Bessboroughs a town house in Cavendish Square, and a villa at Roehampton. Finally, each had children: the Duchess, two daughters, Georgiana and Harriet Cavendish, and a son, the Marquess of Hartington, familiarly known as "Hart"; Lady Bessborough, three sons, John William, William, and Frederick Ponsonby, and, in 1785, a daughter Caroline.

CHAPTER TWO

We turn to the letters, diaries, and biographies of the late eighteenth century, and as they create with their undying power that various and glittering throng, and the whole prospect of that age comes crowding on our sight, we look in vain for a trace of the figure that, as the crowd sweeps by, is to grow to clearer and clearer outline, and to shine forth at last, the beautiful *ignis fatuus* of the coming era.

There is practically no information about the little girl born in 1785, and what there is, is unhappily contradictory. Sir John Ponsonby, in *The Ponsonby Family* says in his chapter on Lady Caroline, "Some writers have maintained that from the age of three to that of nine, she was brought up in Italy under the care of a servant. There appears to be absolutely no foundation for this story. Both her mother, Lady Duncannon, and her grandmother, Lady Spencer, were devoted to the child, and she was brought up entirely under their care." Lady Caroline herself told her friend Lady Morgan that she was in Italy from four till nine years old. As Lady Bessborough constantly visited Italy, it is probable that she took her daughter for protracted visits in that country, which would account for the mistake, if, setting aside the statement of Lady Caroline as valueless, mistake we are to call it.

At a period which it is difficult to decide upon, but probably before her tenth year, she went for a time to a school in Hans Place, kept by Miss Rowden, who had been a governess in the Bessborough family, and had published a poem, dedicated to Lady Bessborough—on "The Pleasures of Friendship":

> *Visions of early youth, ere yet ye fade,*
> *Let my light pen arrest your fleeting shade—*

and a great deal more in the same style. Miss Rowden's previous connection with the family was no doubt responsible for Lady Caroline's being sent to the school. The latter once told Lady Morgan that she had suffered much in her childhood when staying in Italy from the severity of a governess called "Fanny." Miss Rowden's name being

Frances gives rise to the idea that she might have been the dragon, but the account we have of her from other pupils suggests that she was a very amiable school-mistress. Besides Lady Caroline Ponsonby, the school boasted two eminent pupils, both of whom have left some account of it, though neither, unfortunately, was there with Lady Caroline herself; of these, Fanny Kemble and Mary Russell Mitford, the former has left an excellent description in *Recollections of a Girlhood*. Fanny Kemble, daughter of the great John Kemble and niece of Mrs. Siddons, was sent to the school when Miss Rowden, then styled "Mrs." Rowden, had removed it to Paris and settled in the Rue Angoulême. It sounds to have been a remarkably intelligent and liberal establishment, from which many modern girls' schools might take a hint; and, although Mrs. Rowden felt obliged to draw the line at the girls acting *Roxelane*, bursting in upon the rehearsal with, "May, commang! maydemosels, je suis atonnay! May, commang! Kesse ke say! Vous permattay maydemosels être lay filles d'ung seraglio! . . . je vous defang! Je suis biang atonnay!" and sweeping off with the prompt copy, yet they rallied themselves under this reverse, and had great fun with *Andromaque*, though it was a choice, as Fanny Kemble said, which certainly could not be "accused of levity," and though Fanny herself, up to all the professional devices, made them sick before the performance with swallowing raw eggs to clear the voice.

Miss Mitford, whose career at the school was from 1798 to 1802, and therefore during the Hans Place era, leaves in her *Literary Recollections* one or two sketches, which support the impression that it was the sort of school which would have suited Lady Caroline as far as any school could suit her, without becoming totally unsuited to the rest of the pupils.

At the age of nine, however, owing to Lady Bessborough's ill health, she was transferred to the much more questionable surroundings of Devonshire House, where her chief companions were Georgiana and Harriet, whom she wanted to love, but who disliked and criticised her, and Hart, whose early felt and constant devotion perhaps atoned for the coldness of the little girls. "My kind aunt Devonshire took me," she told Lady Morgan, and when one reads her account in the same letter of the domestic arrangements of the Duchess, one cannot but think that Lady Caroline's own negligence and indifference in later years was, at least in part, a result of this period of her upbringing.

Nothing, indeed, could be more natural than that she should be profoundly influenced by the régime of Devonshire House. She was devoted to her mother, and the Duchess was that mother's devoted sister; and though in 1795 the latter's beauty was no doubt on the wane, and she had attained that voluptuous outline which gave rise to the saying that "she always appeared a little larger than life size," her charm was as great as ever: that "flowing good nature" praised by Horace Walpole, combined with the fact that she was still the most important woman in London society, from whose all-night parties the Prince Regent staggered dead drunk at six o'clock in the morning, must have given her the popularity of an easy-going mistress of a household and the influence of a great lady. Lady Morgan has made an abstract in her journal of information given her by Lady Caroline: "She gave curious anecdotes of high life . . . children served on silver, but carrying their plates to the kitchen: no one to attend to them, servants all at variance." The children were ignorant of everything. They knew of no intervening ranks of society between dukes and beggars; they could not think how bread and butter were made, and wondered if horses fed on beef.

In these lavish and haphazard surroundings Lady Caroline, aged ten, was left to do very much as she liked. Her grandmother, Lady Spencer, alarmed at her excitability, had had her examined by Dr. Warren, who said that although there were no symptoms of insanity, she should not be taught anything or placed under any restraint. It seems a curious method of treatment to have recommended in the circumstances, and one which, though it might have answered in the country, might equally well have proved fatal in the vertiginous glitter of Devonshire House. We get at last a definite glimpse of the wild and lovely creature, which can best be conveyed in her own words:

"My mother, having boys, wished ardently for a girl, and I, who evidently ought to have been a soldier, was found a naughty girl, forward, talking, like Richard III [i.e. the Duke of York in *Richard III*]. My instinct, for we all have instincts—was for music—in it I delighted. I cried when it was pathetic, and did all that Dryden's Ode made Alexander do;—of course, I was not allowed to follow it up. My angel mother's ill health prevented my living at home; my kind aunt Devonshire took me; the present Duke [i.e. Hart] loved me better than himself and everyone paid me those compliments shown to children who are precious to their parents or delicate and likely to die."

When she was thirteen she had chicken-pox, and since she seems, for a time at least, to have been at home with her mother, we have Lady Bessborough's account of her convalescence in a letter to Lord Granville Leveson-Gower.

"Caroline has been up half the day; she will not be marked. At least there are only two spots I have doubts of, but they would not do her much harm even if they stayed. . . . She said this morning, 'I suppose Lord Granville would not deign to look at me if I am all pitted with the chicken-pox.' I asked her why she thought so; she said 'he seems too fine a gentleman to like ugly people, but I can assure him I would not give sixpence for anybody who would not like me as well with a rough face as with a smooth one.' I don't know why Caroline supposes you are so governed by looks, but I think you ought to be flattered, as you are certainly the only person she has enquired after. . . . Poor Willy has caught the chicken-pox. I suppose it will go through the family. . . . I never saw anything so pretty as Caroline nursing him."

It must have been much more comfortable having chicken-pox with Lady Bessborough at Roehampton than it would have been with the Duchess at Devonshire House, in spite of the fact that the celebrated Sir Walter Farquhar was the physician to the latter establishment; but she returned there on her recovery and continued her peculiar existence.

The result of Dr. Warren's treatment was that until fifteen she learned nothing. "I wrote not, spelt not, but I wrote verses which they all thought beautiful. For myself, I preferred washing a dog or polishing a piece of Derby-shire spar, or breaking in a horse, to any accomplishment in the world." Though afterwards she developed an exquisite taste in dress, she adds that at this time "drawing-rooms (shall I say withdrawing-rooms as they say now?), looking glasses, finery or dress company were my abhorrence."

Monsieur Rabbe, writing at the end of the last century, says that she toasted muffins for the Duke of Devonshire in his library while he instructed her in politics: an anecdote one would gladly believe, but he gives no authority for it. At all events, she developed a precocious interest in Whig politics, and would drink confusion to the

Tories in mugs of milk;[1] and it was this early passion for the principles of Whiggism which, as will appear later, first aroused her interest in her future husband.

The portrait of the child is, as usual, the sketch for that of the woman. The boyish element in her tastes survived in her fondness for games, her skill as a horsewoman, her habit of dressing herself as a boy, and that finely pointed direction of speech which gives her utterances their inexpressible charm. The sensibility of the child who cried when music was pathetic, and the ardent enthusiasm that fell in love with "a friend of Charles Fox, a friend of liberty"—these make the story.

[1] M.D., British Museum. Obituary notice.

CHAPTER THREE

The three well-known portraits of Lady Caroline Ponsonby—the painting by Finden, one by Hoppner, and the miniature given by her to John Murray—form an interesting study, and explain why some people declared her to be not pretty at all—Galt says that Byron was ashamed to have been in love with her for that reason—and others thought her remarkably pretty. All three pictures show the round head, pointed chin, and large, speaking eyes. The small and beautifully finished head, the exquisite mouth, the fair hair cut short and curled above the ears in a style of such elegant artlessness and sophisticated simplicity, form a strange background for that air of wild intelligence and that look of brilliant happiness on the verge of tears.

There are several contemporary descriptions of her; the obituary notice in the *Literary Gazette*, attributed to Lord Melbourne, says of her appearance that "in person she was small, slight and perfectly formed," but that "her countenance had no other beauty than that of expression—*that* charm it possessed to a singular degree. Her eyes were dark, but her hair and complexion fair." She thus exhibited the rare and striking combination of two very distinct types, inheriting the fair hair of the Ponsonbys and her mother's large dark eyes. Lady Morgan says that she was tall, but this statement is qualified by the fact that Lady Morgan herself was only four feet high; she says also "her face was grave," and that may well have been by the time Lady Morgan made her acquaintance. One of her chief attractions was her voice; the all-powerful Whig aristocracy had its own pronunciation; the forms of "Haryot" for Harriet, "chaney" for china, "yaller," "cowcumber," and so on have come down to us, but Devonshire House had even its own intonation; a nasal drawl, commented on acidly by the débutante Miss Milbanke, who said "Lady Caroline ba-a-a-as like a little sheep"; but some people forgave this. "Her voice," said Lady Morgan, "was soft, low and caressing . . . at once a beauty and a charm, and worked much of that fascination that was peculiarly hers; it softened down her enemies in the moment that they listened to her." Its thrilling quality was further enhanced by a slight lisp. On one occasion when William Harness was dancing with her at Devonshire House, she lifted her petticoat and said, "Gueth how many pairth of thilk thtockingth I have on?" Mr. Harness becoming flustered, she informed him "Thixth." If she were telling the truth, perhaps she had anticipated the criticisms of Byron, who said that her figure wanted that "roundness," for the absence of which mere elegance and grace would never compensate.

The Hoppner portrait seems to have been painted about the time of her marriage, that by Finden some time after, judging by the dress. In that very interesting collection of Byron relics, the property of Lord Gorrell exhibited at Messrs. Bumpus's in August 1931 was a set of porcelain pipes, the work of a German Byromaniac, arranged like the spokes of a wheel in a velvet case; on the bowl of each pipe was painted a portrait of one of Byron's ladies. Lady Caroline is represented by a copy of the Finden portrait, with the dress coloured dark green and the ribbon over her shoulders a bright puce colour. The same exhibition contained the miniature given to John Murray, the colouring of which is so striking that, familiar as the picture is in reproduction, the beholder feels when he sees the original that he has never before had any idea of it. It undoubtedly expresses one of those happiest moments, one of those radiant looks which made people think that the face which "had no charm but that of expression" was actually lovely. She stands against an Italian-blue sky, hung with ruddy golden leaves, and is wearing a page's coat of deep violet colour with a high gold collar and epaulettes; her head is turned over her shoulder, and her bright curls, her roseate face, and hazel eyes make an inspired and glowing picture, not the less valuable as a likeness because the likeness only of a moment.

From the time she was sixteen or seventeen, she must have had a remarkably pleasant existence; the distracting extravaganza of life at Devonshire House was by this time merely a background, and she was now in the company of "my own pretty, dearest and best mama." Lady Bessborough was still in her prime, and a delightful companion for a daughter; she inspired a boundless affection in Lady Caroline, although she could not save her from herself. They spent a great deal of time visiting together at the various family houses: at Althorpe, and the Duke of Devonshire's Chatsworth, and less alluring Hardwick. The Duchess, in unwilling attendance on her husband, who was ill, writes from the latter place: "Caro Pon: says Chatsworth is Paradise and this place Hades, and indeed we do wander about like uneasy spirits."

In 1802, when she was seventeen, Lady Bessborough took her to Paris, where she herself had already made the acquaintance, which afterwards developed into something warmer, of the all-conquering Lord Granville Leveson-Gower. Although this nobleman married, in 1809, Lady Bessborough's niece, Lady Harriet Cavendish (who wrote to her brother, "I do nothing all day but think what an angel my husband is"), Lady Bessborough continued on the most intimate terms with him, and wrote to him almost daily until her death in 1821.

In 1802, Parisian society was in two strata, that presided over by the beautiful Theresa Cabarrus, who entertained only the gentlemen: and the more conventional division, in which many English ladies were cutting a figure, among whom was that notable matchmaker, the Duchess of Gordon.

This lady had made herself very unpopular in the Devonshire House circle; she was a Tory, but that alone would have made her merely negligible; she had, however, succeeded in seriously injuring a friend of the Duchess, and one only second to the latter in social eminence.

Lady Melbourne, a beautiful and very astute woman, had married in her youth Sir Matthew Lamb, handsome and wealthy, but a man of no family and very little intellect. His father, however, had been a man of considerable ability, had made his fortune as an attorney and married Miss Coke, the heiress of the family to whom he was solicitor; in itself a somewhat remarkable feat, although it was, as Sheridan said, an age when everybody's son married nobody's daughter, and therefore perhaps the opposite held good as well. Sir Matthew Lamb thus inherited a vast fortune, and used to say that he had given his wife back her marriage portion in diamonds. On his father's death he acquired a title. Lady Melbourne with her husband's money and her own powerful personality created by main force a position of influence in the fashionable world; her sons, Peniston and William, were at Harrow, and she was generous and attentive to their schoolfellow, the Prince of Wales, who afterwards repaid her with a gift of his intimate friendship and all its agreeable consequences. When the Duchess of Devonshire began her married life, Lady Melbourne saw a threatened eclipse of herself, and became most friendly with the new luminary over whom she exerted all the influence of an elder woman over a girl, and of a hard nature over a pliant one. Her pains were not thrown away; she excited the Duchess's gushing affection, and her ardent partisanship in private as well as public affairs. Lady Melbourne's most recent lover was the Duke of Bedford, who, it was supposed, would never marry, since his time was fully occupied between Lady Melbourne and the actress, Mrs. Palmer. The Duchess of Gordon's talents as a matchmaker had already been exerted on behalf of three of her five daughters, and with eminent success; but, even so, the world was unprepared for her final coup, which betrothed the hitherto unassailable Duke, and the Whig Duke at that, to her youngest daughter, Lady Georgiana Gordon. Agitated letters, in the Duchess of Devonshire's never very coherent style, poured in upon Lady Melbourne, first refusing to believe such a catastrophe, then picturing, with all the liveliness of exasperation, the Duke joining his relations-in-law in their rustic pastimes, smoking clay pipes and watching "the young one" jumping over the backs of chairs. Everything was put a stop to, however, by the Duke's sudden and unexpected death, upon which the Duchess of Gordon made a fine rally, and married Lady Georgiana to his younger brother. As her activities had displeased the Duchess of Devonshire, she was also in the bad books of Lady Bessborough; however, as she was giving grand balls in Paris to celebrate the engagement, Lady Bessborough said she should call, "for Caro's sake."

She might indeed feel inclined to make more than the ordinary sacrifices of a mother on such occasions, to bring out so striking and unusual a daughter. The waywardness and hoydenism of the child had developed into the charming, unaffected originality of a remarkable woman. "She had no patience, as she said, with preliminaries, and skipped all the prefatory matters continually deemed indispensable, about coming or not coming, health and the weather, which bored her to extinction. To anyone she liked, she gave her hand at a second or third interview, without the least unmaidenly air of freedom, and with anyone whom she did not fancy she would not shake hands at all." Her complete immunity from any contact with what was disreputable, despite the unconventionality of her manner, is shown in the following curious letter of Lady Bessborough to Lord Granville Leveson-Gower.

"If you were here, I know you would feel as indignant as I do, as much puzzled at something which has happened to me, or rather to my Caro. Think of her receiving a letter filled with every gross, disgusting indecency that the most depraved imagination could suggest, worse indeed than anything that I ever heard, saw, or read or could imagine. . . . It is what I am quite convinced you would not believe possible, even supposing it addressed to some woman in the street; think then of writing thus to a girl! She luckily only read a few lines, when she was so shocked that she flew to me, and gave me the horrid letter . . . what adds to our perplexity is, that what is not too nasty and disgusting to look at, is very well written, and alludes to conversations and jokes that passed at my sister's only a few days ago. The letter is written in the name of Mr. Hill, in consequence of her having been told as she was a few nights ago by Georgiana, that he thought her the cleverest and prettiest girl in London. She answered 'Dear Mr. Hill! I shall set about admiring him whenever I meet him'; and two or three times since she has asked her cousins whether her Dear Mr. H. was to be there. This is alluded to in the letter and also some things said by Georgiana. Is it not inconceivable? Poor little soul! She has been quite ill with it. I do think it very hard; there never was a purer, more delicate mind existing than hers. . . . C'est l'innocence de l'Enfance même."

Her personality had already impressed itself on her mother's circle. In her commonplace book, the first page is devoted to a list of the nicknames bestowed upon her—"Ariel," "Sprite," "Savage," "Squirrel." The lively yet serious cast of her character, with her enchanting appearance, and her manner free from all self-consciousness, captivated one of the most lovable, as well as one of the most original, characters of the century. When she was only twelve, she had, she told Lady Morgan, "fallen in love with a friend of Charles Fox, a friend of liberty, whose poems I had read, whose self I had never seen. And when I did see him at thirteen, could I change? No. I was more attached than ever. William Lamb was beautiful, and far the cleverest person then about, and the most daring in his opinions, in his love of liberty and independence. He thought of me but as a child, yet he liked me much."

This meeting took place when Lady Caroline was on a visit, with her Devonshire cousins, to Lady Melbourne at Brocket Hall. She can hardly have thought, when she saw the house on its lawn that slopes down to a river running through the park, how much of her time she was to spend there in later years. The verses she mentions do not appear to have been preserved; they were probably handed about in manuscript; but she copied into her commonplace book his essay "On the Progressive Improvement of Mankind," which he wrote at the age of nineteen, and which had been quoted by Fox in the House. William Lamb did indeed "like her much," and on the occasion of this visit he made the celebrated remark, "Of all the girls of Devonshire House, that is the one for me." In the succeeding years until 1805 he saw more and more of her, visiting at houses where she was, and often a guest at Roehampton. No one seems to have thought seriously of their friendship, for, though in the eyes of posterity Lord Melbourne would make any family illustrious, at this time the Melbournes were neither noble nor distinguished, and, though they were exceedingly wealthy, William Lamb was only the second son. Lady Bessborough no doubt had plans for her daughter, who seemed formed by birth and attractions to make a brilliant match, although she was rather annoying her mother at this time by some "little *sauvageries*" of behaviour. A connection with the Melbournes could not have appeared to Lady Bessborough particularly desirable: besides, she disliked what she took to be the character of William Lamb.

But Lady Caroline showed a singularly perfect taste, and one from which she never in her heart went back; years later, when she had destroyed what might have been one of the happiest and most interesting married lives known to fame, she asked someone, "Who do you think was the finest man I ever knew?" The answer, "Byron," was met with, "No. William Lamb."

It is impossible to describe the fascination of character:

A strange, invisible perfume hits the sense,

and one can but bring together the ingredients, the information contained in anecdote and contemporary opinion, and leave them to exhale their combined essences into the savour of a personality. Fanny Kemble met Lamb as Lord Melbourne, when, an elderly man, he was past the turmoil of his married life.

24

"He was," she says, "an exceedingly handsome man, with a fine person verging towards the portly, and a sweet countenance, more expressive of refined, easy, careless good humour than any face I ever saw. His beauty was of too well-born and well-bred a type to be unpleasantly sensual, but his whole face, person, expression and manner conveyed the idea of a pleasure-loving nature, habitually self-indulgent and indulgent to others. He was my *beau ideal* of an Epicurean philosopher, supposing it possible that an Epicurean philosopher could have consented to be Prime Minister of England."

Lady Bessborough did not care for the young man; she did not like his mother, whom, however, dutiful son as he was, he did not at all resemble; but she saw now that her daughter was irresistibly attracted, and that the childish friendship had been allowed to go too far if she and Lord Bessborough did not mean to consent to a marriage. Unwilling as she was to see the connection, she showed the kindest sympathy mingled with good sense; Caroline was only nineteen, and she belonged to a circle where, if anywhere, personal choice in matrimony is circumscribed by material conditions; it was, moreover, an age when even an affectionate mother would force a daughter's inclination in what was considered by her family to be a suitable match. Of the fierce and adamantine methods of marrying off daughters practised by fashionable women we have some picture in *Whistle Me First*, a play written for private theatricals by William's brother, George, the prologue to which contains the following lines:

> *At night again on us all pleasures pall,*
> *Bid for by inch of candle at a ball,*
> *And, e'en when Fashion's toilsome revels cease,*
> *For us no pause, no liberty, no peace.*
> *For when the matrons speak of suppers small,*
> *"A few choice friends beside ourselves, that's all,"*
> This *language in plain truth they mean to hold,*
> *"A girl, by private contract to be sold."*

But Lady Bessborough's concern was with the personal happiness of her daughter. She writes in 1805 to Lord Granville Leveson-Gower:

"My poor Caroline's fate is probably deciding for ever; I have long

25

foreseen and endeavoured to avoid what has just happened—W. Lamb's proposing to her, but she likes him too much for me to do more than entreat a little further acquaintance on both sides, and not having this declared immediately, which precludes all possibility of retreat." She reviews the situation with considerable broadmindedness. "In some things I like it. He has a thousand good qualities, is very clever, which is absolutely necessary for her; and above all she has preferred him from childhood, and is now so much in love with him that before his speaking, I dreaded its affecting her health. But on the other hand, I dislike the connexion extremely. I dislike his manners, and still more his principles and his creed, or rather no creed. Yet to her his behaviour has been honourable and his letter is beautiful."

William Lamb seems to have "spoken" by letter, or else to have followed a verbal proposal by a written declaration. He wrote:

"I have loved you for four years, loved you deeply, dearly, faithfully, —so faithfully that my love has withstood my firm determination to conquer it when honour forbade my declaring myself—has withstood all that absence, variety of objects, my own endeavours to seek and like others, or to occupy my mind with a fixed attention to my own profession, could do to shake it."

The considerations of honour which forbade his declaring himself were the uncertain nature of his prospects, but the death of his elder brother, Peniston, in 1803 had left him heir to the Melbourne fortune. This sincere and earnest declaration, with the slight glaze of formality on the diction, reminiscent of the previous century, is oddly different from the colloquial, cool, and racy style that we consider characteristic of Lord Melbourne's utterances.

It was the deciding-point in the matter. On Thursday evening Lady Bessborough and Caroline came home very late from Devonshire House. "Entering my room, Caro gave me a letter from W. and throwing her arms round my neck, told me she loved him better than anything but me, but would give him up if I required it." Lady Bessborough was not proof against this, and gave her consent; Lord Bessborough's views are not mentioned, but they must have been understood to be favourable provided his wife was satisfied. "Their love for one another and his behaviour have quite reconciled me to it," the latter wrote to Lord Granville Leveson-Gower: "I do believe all her ill health, and all the little oddities of manner and *sauvageries* that

26

used to vex me arose from the unhappiness that was constantly preying upon her."

The secret was confined to the immediate family for a day or two. Caroline could not bear "W" even to come to the house till everything was quite settled, but she arranged to meet him at Drury Lane, and Lady Bessborough gives the following account of the evening:

"I never saw anything so warm and animated as his manner towards her, and of course he soon succeeded in obtaining every promise he wished. I had not seen him to speak to, and he followed me into the passage behind the box. I was very nervous, and on telling him that I knew Lord B. joined with me in leaving everything to Caro's decision, he answered, 'And that decision is in my favour, thank heaven!' and so saying, threw his arms round me and kissed me. At that very moment, I saw *the Pope* (Canning) and Mr. Hammond before me in the utmost astonishment." William Lamb saw them too, took fright, and darted away down the stairs, while Lady Bessborough, distressed at the idea of a misunderstanding, flew after Mr. Canning and explained the circumstances; upon which he was delighted, praised William Lamb "excessively," and altogether "did her more good than anything she had heard before."

This agreeable interlude was fortunate, for a sad scene awaited them. The Duke of Devonshire had for a long time wanted Lady Caroline to marry the Marquis of Hartington, who was now seventeen and whose boyish affection, like her own for William Lamb, had ripened into genuine passion. Ignorant of what had been happening, the Duke chose this juncture for mentioning the matter to Lady Bessborough; the disclosure was now inevitable, and when Lady Bessborough and Caroline called in at Devonshire House after the theatre, there was a tragic interview with "poor Hart," who went into violent hysterics, reproached Caroline bitterly, saying that he had always wanted to make her his wife when he should be eighteen, and carried on to such an extent that it became necessary to send for Sir Walter Farquhar.

In the meantime, Lady Melbourne appeared to be prospering. Not only was her son on the verge of so advantageous a marriage, but her daughter, Emily, was about to be married to Lord Cowper of Althorpe. A double connection of the families was thus formed; Lord Cowper was the grandson of Lady Spencer and first cousin of Lady Caroline. Emily Lamb is known to history as Lady Palmerston, and consequently

27

enjoys the reputation of one of the most interesting and charming of the Victorian great ladies; but she was fifty at the time of her marriage to Palmerston, and the first half of her life presents an aspect oddly at variance with the reputation assigned to her in later years. In the first place, she was reputed to be Palmerston's mistress before the death of Lord Cowper permitted her to marry him: a fact ignored in the discreeter memoirs of the later period, but pointed out by the egregious Greville. Secondly, the qualities of benevolence, virtue, and dignity, for which in the former works she is so continuously celebrated, seem to have developed rather late in life—coincidently with the birth of the Victorian era. All this is of course quite within the bounds of probability; it would be a dismal thing if at fifty we could show no improvement on ourselves at nineteen. But, to anyone who only knows Lady Palmerston through the medium of highly laudatory biography, the following comments of Lady Bessborough may cause a slight surprise; the latter, a few years after Emily's marriage, was bringing out Harriet Cavendish, as the Duchess of Devonshire was too ill to undertake the labour. "Emily is pretty, but whether from her having done me mischief, or fact, I know not, but she does not seem to me good natured— or sincere. She flatters Harriet violently to her face, and takes every opportunity of cutting at her. Though I do not think Harriet handsome, she is not ugly: as that is a mere matter of opinion, I should say nothing at her being called so. Emily chooses to add to ugliness, her being the greatest gull that ever was, and what she calls dull and stupid; this most certainly is not true; and poor Harriet thinks all the while that Emily dotes on her."

Despite the drawbacks of ill nature and insincerity, Emily Lamb was very attractive; she was also devoted to Lady Melbourne, and in many ways a faithful reflection of her mother. When she was married and gone to Panshanger, Lady Melbourne prepared to receive, in place of her dutiful and doting daughter, a bird of very different plumage.

The Melbournes had disinterestedly obliged the Prince Regent by exchanging houses with him, leaving their mansion—on what is now the site of Albany, and which had been furnished at great expense—for his house in Whitehall, which is now the Scottish Office, and anyone walking past the Horse Guards must pass through the pillars of its portico, for they stand at the edge of the pavement. From the opposite pavement it can be seen that the portico is topped by a great leaded dome, behind which rises the top storey of the house, a plain brick front with a concealed roof and square sash windows. Inside the main door is the hall, with its black and white flags and large staircase ascending from it.

The big rooms of the ground floor were retained by Lady Melbourne, while the upper floors were fitted up for Mr. William and Lady Caroline Lamb.

On May 8th, said Lady Bessborough, "The Prince of Wales and Farquhar had been informed [the latter, no doubt, when he came to attend "poor Hart"], and Lord B. having received and accepted a formal proposal, all London came to wish me joy." She said the house was full of milliners and mantua-makers, and she had her hands full with preparations. On June 2nd everything was ready. Lady Elizabeth Foster wrote to Augustus, then an attaché at Washington:

"Caroline Ponsonby is to be married to-morrow. She looks prettier than ever I saw her. Sometimes she is very nervous, but in general she appears to be very happy. William Lamb seems quite devoted to her." On the previous evening, she continued, they had all had supper at Devonshire House, and Caroline had received her wedding presents. Her cousin Georgiana's husband, Lord Morpeth, gave her "a beautiful æqua marina clasp;" Harriet Cavendish "a beautiful burnt-topaz cross," an ornament which must have suited her to perfection. Lady Elizabeth herself gave her a pearl cross with a diamond in the centre. Her father-in-law, Lord Melbourne, gave her a set of amethysts, and Lady Melbourne a diamond wreath; while the Duke of Devonshire presented her with her wedding dress, of which, unfortunately, no description remains, and the Duchess with a jewelled wreath. Lady Elizabeth does not mention any offering from poor Hart; perhaps she overlooked it, or perhaps he was too much distressed to choose a wedding present.

Despite her adoration of William, the kindness of everybody, the celebrations at Devonshire House, and the wedding presents, Caroline was not altogether happy. Lady Bessborough had taken her to Roehampton the Sunday before the wedding, and wrote to Lord Granville Leveson-Gower that "in the evening, she was rather low and frightened." William was with them, and Lady Bessborough encouraged her by reminding her that to seem unhappy might hurt his feelings.

"She turned round to him and said, 'My dear William, judge what my love must be, when I can leave such a mother as this for you. Girls who are not happy at home may marry without regret, but it required very strong affection indeed to overpower mine.' I believe I told you this before, but it made such a strong impression on me from her eager manner of saying it, and the extreme kindness of his answer to her and to me; indeed I am so flattered by my children, it will turn my head."

The wedding took place in Cavendish Square on June 3rd, at eight o'clock in the evening; the party consisting of the Ponsonbys, Devonshires, the Melbournes, Lady Elizabeth Foster, the Morpeths, Lady Spencer and her son and grandson, Lord Spencer, and Lord Althorpe.

According to a statement made in after years by Lady Caroline herself, she had a hysterical outburst and tore her wedding dress to pieces. Lady Elizabeth, however, in giving Augustus an account of the ceremony, merely says "She was dreadfully nervous," and adds, "His manner to her was beautiful, so tender and considerate."

At nine o'clock they set off in the carriage and drove through the summer evening to the greenery and quiet of Hertfordshire. People born in that county think that nowhere is summer more beautiful than among those towering elm trees and great oaks, those meadows white with daisies and ethereal with may. At night the scent and dew hang in the stillness, until a faint night wind thrills the grass, and the air stirs with odour and murmuring sound.

It must have been dark by the time they drove into the park with its silent trees.

Years afterwards Lady Caroline recalled "those principles I came to William with, that horror of vice, of deceit, of anything that was the least improper; that religion I believed in without a doubt . . . the almost childlike innocence and inexperience I had preserved till then."

CHAPTER FOUR

The present idea of a secluded honeymoon seems to have been un-fashionable a hundred years ago, when a sister of the bride frequently accompanied the couple on their journey. This was all in favour of Lady Caroline, as a visit from her mother could be managed without the air of anything unusual.

Lady Bessborough wrote to her correspondent a few days after the marriage to say that the next day she was going to Brocket; but, pre-cipitate as the visit seems to-day, it was only postponed so long be-cause, she said, "Poor little Caro has been ill, and would see nobody, not even me, until to-day. I am just going."

In the delicate and highly strung frame of Lady Caroline Lamb, happiness beyond a certain degree of intensity became, perhaps, an agitation which could hardly be distinguished from suffering. She might not know whether she were happy or unhappy, but she knew that she was wretchedly ill. Yet even this state of affairs was no doubt interesting to William Lamb; he may have found a curious pleasure in witnessing the distraction of which he was the cause, and preserved a tender and watchful equanimity, waiting for her to realise their hap-piness.

But Lady Bessborough, though admitting that "she never saw any-thing so kind as he was," was distressed at her daughter's condition. "Really, being married is a state of great suffering to a girl in every way. I do think it very hard that men should always have *beau jeu* on all occasions, and that all pain, *Morale et Physique*, should be re-served for us."

But Lady Caroline got better; the long summer days in Brocket Park, the company of her mother, and the exquisite tact and patience of her husband gradually restored the tone of her nerves. They passed the chief of the day out of doors, and the ladies spent the evening drawing while William Lamb read aloud to them. In a few days Lady Bessborough felt able, and perhaps anxious, to leave them, and re-turned to Roehampton, and thence to London. At the former she missed Caroline sorely, the more so as the house was still sounding with merry-making in celebration of the wedding. "The Servants' Hall," she wrote, "are footing it away for her, and I conclude getting very drunk, as I heard my health this moment drank with three loud cheers. All this gaiety does not make me feel the less forlorn without her, but she is so happy, it would be very selfish not to feel so also."

On her return to London, which heralded that of the bridal pair themselves, Lady Bessborough went to pay a call on Lady Melbourne. She had previously confided to Lord Granville Leveson-Gower, "I like William above all things, but I could dispense with some of his *entours*. But this I must not even whisper." Who one of the "*entours*" might be, it is not difficult to guess. "I went to Whitehall last night, but somehow or other I am not comfortable. 'The Thorn,' though she seemed delighted with the marriage, has had throughout a degree of sharpness towards me that is very unpleasant to me. Yesterday, after some very unpleasant cuts, she told me she hoped the daughter would turn out better than the mother, or William might have to repent of his choice, and would not, like many husbands, be made to repent *impunément*." That Lady Bessborough should have borne with this impertinence, and from Lady Melbourne of all people, is only another indication of what a mother will put up with in order to keep all smooth with her daughter's new relations. Her reply was a miracle of reticence. "I . . . only said I hoped and believed she would prove much better, especially, I added, with the help of your advice. (I would not say '*example*'.)"

She may have shrunk from the idea of Caroline's going immediately to live under the unsympathetic auspices of The Thorn. At all events, when the Lambs returned to town, they came first of all to Cavendish Square, where Lady Bessborough had made them "a very comfortable apartment." Caroline was well, and in spirits, but her mother could not help exclaiming, "So unlike a wife—it is more like a school girl." Augustus Foster wrote from Washington: "I cannot imagine Lady Caroline married. How changed she must be! The delicate Ariel, the little Fairy Queen, become a wife, and soon, perhaps, a mother!" Lady Elizabeth replied that he need not distress himself: "She is still the same wild, delicate, odd, delightful person, unlike everything."

Like a schoolgirl, or unlike everything, but she now occupied a position of the most worldly importance, in what the age called the first circles, and in the height of *ton*. There are no descriptions of her trousseau, the toilets whose preparation had filled the house with milliners and mantua-makers a few months ago; but a page or two out of *La Belle Assemblée*, the oracle of fashion, tell us what was worn in general in this restricted circle, and prescribe the limits within which the dress of such an *élégante* must have appeared. Her hair was exactly correct; *La Belle Assemblée* dictated that it should be "cropped close behind and in dishevelled curls in front." Lady Caroline's complexion, fair and pale, was also in accordance with the ideas of *La Belle Assemblée*, although the paper was broadminded on this point. "It is so much the fashion to look pale now that you may buy a pot of rouge for half a crown . . . and first-rates use a sort of lotion to promote that interesting shade of the lily which has of late subdued the rose." But while recognising the disuse of rouge among first-rates, the writer hopes "not to see this animating appendage to the toilet entirely exploded." From which it would seem that the language of fashion-books never has had very much affinity with that of ordinary speech. The renaissance of Greek forms in the early nineteenth century, which filled houses with tea-caddies shaped like urns, classical-looking tables, collections of coins, marble mantelpieces like the porch of a temple, and applied flat Grecian porticoes to their fronts of English red brick, had an even more thoroughgoing influence on female dress; at the beginning of the century, when the craze was at its height, a lady's toilet, including shoes, was said to weigh eight ounces; petticoats were damped to cling tightly to the figure, and the dress, or "robe," consisted of one scanty, high-waisted, low-bosomed, sleeveless garment, from which gradually evolved the pretty "Regency" style, with its similar outline but a fuller skirt and short puffed sleeves. The mania for extreme delicacy persisted; in 1805 *La Belle Assemblée* describes the dresses at a fashionable function: "Not a few beautiful and elegant figures were attired in dresses of cloud-coloured crêpe or transparent muslin, whose filmy texture, changing in hue and shade from the ever-varying folds of their gossamer drapery, seemed to wrap the elegant wearers in robes of light, impalpable ether." All thick materials for outdoor wear, and all furs except ermine, were declared impossible, "the yielding and adhesive imperial satin of gossamer softness" was the ideal medium for pelisses and spencers. "White and rose-coloured silk stockings with a narrow clock, unembroidered, are the only stockings worn," announces the same authority; shoes were made usually of satin or silk, in white, yellow, turquoise, green, or pink, though one

33

pair is described of striped lilac kid; there was some variety in head-gear, between bonnets with wide, lace-filled brims and stove-pipe hats tied under the chin; one costume is completed by "a white satin mortar-board, the tassel a rich bunch of small strung pearls," while for theatres and operas a semicircular handkerchief of net, with a scalloped edge bordered with lace, was placed over one side of the head.

Lady Caroline, as one of the first-rates, had the fashionable taste for diaphanous muslin dresses; later she shocked the less fashionable Fanny Burney with her vaporous drapery; she also had a strong in-dividual taste, which included a leaning towards masculine costume. *The Memoirs of a Female Dandy*, written about 1810, describes the heroine's going about without a tremor in elegant male attire, though she burst into tears when the ladies left the opera-box on the ground that they couldn't sit with a "kept mistress." Such masculinity was perhaps only skin deep, and assumed for the most feminine purposes. But Lady Caroline Lamb was not artful; a girl who at the age of thirteen thinks that the world is composed of dukes and beggars thinks so, how-ever odd her surroundings, because she does not care how it is com-posed at all. The startling nature of her behaviour has been criticised as "exhibitionism," but a study of her early environment would sug-gest that it was the very reverse: a complete indifference to public opinion, or, rather, no consciousness of that opinion's existence. She had her own standards, but they were not concerned with the externals of behaviour, which are all that public comment is busied with.

"Wild, delicate, odd, delightful:" with her elegance, her erudition, her inconsequent humour, her "horror of vice, of deceit, of anything that was in the least improper," her person and her mind were alike grateful to the Epicurean taste of William Lamb.

At first his choice seemed fully justified; he was exquisitely happy. He and Caroline were observed "to flirt all day"; at night they went to balls and parties, or flung open the double doors of their suite in Mel-bourne House to a rout, the line of whose waiting carriages extended from Whitehall to the Admiralty Arch.

A feature of their *ménage* were the little pages Lady Caroline employed, whose costumes she sometimes borrowed when she felt inclined; her slight figure and her short hair made it a simple thing for her to "obscure" herself in "the lovely garnish of a boy." She was very particular as to their clothes, and in the British Museum is a letter to

34

her tailor, Mr. Baker, containing instructions, and illustrated by her pencil drawings of a child, front view and back, and hastily painted in scarlet and sepia water-colour. She said "the red cloth waistcoat and the drab must have three rows of buttons, and the drab waistcoat red down the seams and button holes: they must both be made to button close up to the neck cloth and a drab belt with red seams and buttons made to go to either; the jacket you made is not quite a proper shape, not sloped off enough on the side before, and the belt and waistcoat near an inch and a half too long-waisted, the trousers also too tight at the bottom, and too short, so that they are not concealed as they should be under the belt. This does not signify for what has been done hitherto, but I wish you to attend to it in future."

Lady Caroline was not only in the midst of every social distraction; she was also within easy distance of her mother in Cavendish Square; nearer still to her kind aunt Devonshire; and, secure in the protection of her husband, she could ignore the ground floor of Melbourne House. William Lamb, in the possession of this fairy-like creature whom he had pursued for four years, and who now adored him with the intensity of passion and of youth, can have had, with wealth and the prospect of an interesting political career, hardly the ability to form a wish.

And yet there were faint signs of coming trouble. William's indolence, always a severe trial to his ambitious mother, prevented his occupying himself with any seriousness in a parliamentary career; he echoed the sentiment of his father-in-law, who had declined the post of Postmaster-General, and later that of Lord Steward, observing that "a place is convenient, but independence is much pleasanter." He had, besides, an absorbing preoccupation; not only that of the ordinary young husband in a young and charming wife; he was savouring a rare pleasure in deflowering, even while he admired, the wild innocence, the barbaric purity, of the creature who had been brought up, an uncontaminated savage, in the splendour and corruption of Devonshire House. With her quick intelligence and the influence her love and his own superior wisdom gave him, the conducting of her worldly education was a delightful task, and was she not even more fascinating when she at last became companionable to a man of the world? She said: "he called me prudish, said I was strait-laced and amused himself with instructing me in things I need never have known."

Another circumstance threatening their happiness was showing itself, in the fragility of Lady Caroline's nerves; she was, probably, though happy, constantly on the point of exhaustion, and the splendid dissipations in which she engaged—her father-in-law called her "Your Lavish-ship"—counteracted the soothing influence of her husband's presence. They were hardly settled in Melbourne House before Lady Bessborough had her hands full. Her sister was lying ill at Devonshire House, in the first stages of the disease of which she was soon to die, and now Caroline succumbed to some nervous disorder, and took to her bed "in sad pain." "I run between the two," said poor Lady Bessborough; one of her worst trials was the condition of the Duchess's financial affairs. The Duke appears to have resigned from the position, and left his sister-in-law, who, it is only fair to remember, had been a participator in the Duchess's extravagances, to deal with the matter as best she could. "I [am] drove mad with every day hearing some fresh claim on my Sis: whose affairs are to be put into my hands, as the only person she will entirely trust, and the Duke says he has so high an opinion of my integrity that if I will give him my word that no new debts shall be entered into, and that I tell him the whole sum to my knowledge, he will trust implicitly to me, and not enquire the names or circumstances, but you cannot think how worrying this is!"

However, a modus was arrived at with the creditors; the Duchess made a temporary improvement; and Lady Bessborough's next care was that of superintending the wedding of her eldest son, Lord Duncannon, to Lady Maria Fane.

That Lord Duncannon was a man of warmer feeling than his portrait suggests, exceedingly handsome though it be, is indicated by the fact that he was one of the few Governor-Generals of Ireland whose retirement was regretted by the Irish themselves; he had the interesting public duty of laying out Hyde Park and Regent's Park, and his name survives in Duncannon Street and the Duncannon Arms. His sister left her mark on nothing so solid, and yet he must now be carefully read up, while she comes to life with every mention of her name.

Lady Maria, the daughter of Lord Bathurst, was a good-looking and worthy girl, but somewhat slow, in comparison, at least, with the mother- and sister-in-law with whom she was to be connected. But Lady Bessborough appeared, as usual, to unite the susceptibility to cares and agitations of a human being with the disposition of an angel. She wrote to Lord Granville Leveson-Gower that the bride "told me this morning she should not mind going; and when I carried her my diamonds etc., she threw her arms round my neck and said, 'I do not wonder at Lady Caroline's being miserable at leaving you; for I have already received more kindness from you than I ever did from my own family'! Do not say this."

The Ponsonby sensibility, of which Lady Caroline had so overflowing a share, appeared even in Lord Duncannon at this crisis; his mother thought him "very nervous," especially just before the ceremony, though she adds that they all behaved very well. The couple went off at once to Roehampton, where they were to have an apartment, just as Lady Caroline was established under the Melbourne roof. The new Lady Duncannon bore her happiness better than the former. Two days afterwards Lady Bessborough writes: "I have heard of *les Mariés*; she behaves better than Caroline. . . . I really hope that they will be very happy, and that she will attach herself to me and love me like a daughter. I shall always treat her as if she really was my own, but when I hear Lady Duncannon spoken of, I turn round and think it is me!"

She soon needed all the affection her own sweetness had inspired. In 1806 the Duchess of Devonshire died. Her death was in a sense a national loss, as if a picture or statue had been destroyed; but to her sister it was a blow from which she never recovered. Years after it had occurred she visited the vault at Chatsworth, meaning to lay some flowers on the tomb; but the keeper had to take them from her and go down into the vault with them, while she knelt on the floor above, over the spot where the coffin lay; and when, again long after, she dreamed of her sister, she would start up, awaking "with every wound torn open afresh." But she had her children, and of these Caroline was perhaps the most dear; she called for the most attention and anxiety; though at present all was going well. When they were not together, Caroline wrote to her, describing her amusements. The theatre was a favourite one, though William Lamb was critical. Greville went with him, when he was Prime Minister, to a performance of *Everyman in his Humour*, at which he exclaimed loudly, "I knew this play would be dull, but that it would be so damned dull as this I did not suppose." However, he accompanied his wife, although not punctually. Lady Elizabeth Foster had, it boots not to enquire how, a daughter known as Mademoiselle Caroline Rosalie St. Jules; the marriage of this young lady to George Lamb accounted for Lady Caroline's appellation of

37

Caro William, to distinguish her from Caro George. A letter to Lady Bessborough describes a theatre-party during the second Caroline's engagement; in it Lady Caroline says:

"I could not help remarking the difference between a husband and a lover! George had been an hour and a half at the play before William appeared, who, when he came, I must say was very agreeable, and infinitely more entertaining than Lord Stair—I am so poetical that it is a mercy I do not write my letters like Dolly, the cook's maid. Perhaps I should if I had a little more time. If Lady D. is with child, the jokes about Pemberton will be endless, as we both consulted him at the same time to make us so, and he has the reputation of being infallible.

"(I must just go and fetch a watch. I will be back in a minute.)

"Lady Melbourne sent you many kind messages yesterday, and invited you here, which considering her knowledge of your expedition to Holywell was more kind than well-judged.

"God bless my own, pretty, dearest and best mama. I will write again tomorrow. In the meantime, believe me, most truly, most affectionately, and dutifully,

"Caro Lamb."

Dr. Pemberton's reputation for infallibility was once more justified. Lady Elizabeth wrote to Augustus, who seems to have been in receipt of all the news: "Caroline Lamb is with child, but her uncertain health prevents one's knowing what is her state, or almost what to hope." She continued to go about, however, and in August sent Lady Bessborough an amusing account of a dinner-party in the neighbourhood of Brocket.

"I was . . . sat down to play Loo with the Controller of the Customs, the Parson of the Parish, Lord Henry Seymour, and the doctor, who all quarrelled about how I should play; and to my inexpressible horror and amazement I heard Lord Henry vehemently assert that Lady Caroline *should* play her trumps when she pleased and without acquainting the Public, and should say 'Pam, be civil,' according to the old Walpole way of playing it.

"The Controller of the Customs warmly maintained that Lady Caroline Lamb *must* play a trump if she had one in her hand, though it might prove her own perdition.

"Words grew high, and I grew frightened, when they all turned on me and asked if I had ever played at Loo before.

" 'Yes,' I replied, 'at the Princess's, last night.'

" 'And what sort of Loo was that?' they said eagerly. 'What sort of Loo?'

" 'A very different one,' I answered, and they all eagerly asked me in what respect.

" 'A much quieter one,' I said, and this for a moment made them all laugh, but after a time it broke out again worse than ever, and they began to argue who was right, which put them all in a worse rage than before. After a few rounds I was glad enough to get home."

Towards the end of the month, she was in Whitehall and no longer felt able to leave the house. Lady Bessborough remained with her in great anxiety; she tried to distract Caroline by reading aloud *The Beggar Girl* to her, while outside, the rain poured down in torrents. On the night of August 28th, her cares were suspended by a most indecorous interruption. Sheridan, whom one can hardly dissociate from *The Rivals* and *The School for Scandal*, had written his last play in 1799, and, though he still owned and managed Drury Lane till its destruction by fire in 1809, his career for the last sixteen years of his life was one of political importance, and, owing to his friendship with the Prince of Wales, social success. His wife, the beautiful Miss Linley, had died in 1792, and he had married Esther Ogle, known to the Devonshire House circle as Hecca. Lady Bessborough was disturbed at Caroline's bedside by a note from Hecca, begging her to come instantly. Lady Bessborough hardly knew what to do, but sent a note in reply saying that she would come when Caroline was settled for the night. At midnight she drove to the Sheridans' apartment, where she found Sheridan extremely drunk, protesting that she was his only love; his wife's naïve surprise at this suggests that she was a stranger to the circle into which she had married. The scene became so painful that it was only by having Sheridan locked into his room that Lady Bessborough could make her escape. The next day was one of great suspense; Caroline had begun to be ill, but "so slow and lingering" that they could not tell what to think. On the next evening, however, a note was sent to Lord Granville Leveson-Gower: "Caroline has given birth to a very fine boy; I am too happy and too tired to

39

write any more to-night, but you, I am sure, will be glad of anything that makes me so."

Lady Caroline's pleasure in the baby was intense: she wrote in her commonplace book:

> *His little eyes like William's shine—*
> *How great is then my joy,*
> *For while I call this darling mine,*
> *I see 'tis William's boy.*

The interest in the event was widespread; Lord Castlereagh sent to know if Lady Caroline could bear the noise of firing in the oncoming celebrations of the capture of Copenhagen; to which she replied that good news, however announced, could never hurt her. Lady Castlereagh paid a visit of congratulation, and annoyed the proud grandmother by her placid demeanour and her way of talking "with equal indifference of Bombardments and Assemblies, the baby and the furniture, the emptiness of London, the massacre of Buenos Ayres, Lord Castlereagh's increasing debility and the doubtful success of Mr. Greville's Opera."

The christening was like that of a baby in a fairytale; the Prince Regent offered to stand godfather, and Lady Bessborough hied out as far as Charing Cross to buy some respectable writing paper on which to return thanks for the honour; Lord Granville Leveson-Gower had the benefit of a sheet, with apologies for the very shabby stationery which, during the crisis, had been all she had been able to lay her hand on.

Sheridan was very eager to come to the christening-party, principally, no doubt, as it would be an opportunity of pleasing himself and tormenting Lady Bessborough by a meeting. He asked Lady Bessborough and Lady Caroline in turn whether he might come, and they both replied that Lady Melbourne was giving all the invitations. He then attacked Lady Melbourne, who said that the company would be restricted to relatives, and that if she began inviting strangers there would be no end to it. But Sheridan was equal to The Thorn; the evening came, and the company was assembled waiting for the Prince Regent, when the double doors were thrown open, and in came Sheridan, announcing the Prince, and himself as the gentleman attending him. Nothing could be done, and the party proceeded in great state. The outside of Melbourne House was so much illuminated that it looked like a temple, a description readily understandable when one sees the classical porch. Everyone was beautifully dressed, and, though the crowd was great, the size of the rooms prevented discomfort or heat. After supper they sat down to play a paper game, in which each player wrote a verse and handed it to his neighbour, who had to write the answer. Sheridan pressed upon Lady Bessborough the following lines on the baby:

> *Grant Heaven, sweet Babe, thou mayest inherit*
> *What Heaven only can impart,*
> *Thy Father's manly sense and spirit,*
> *Thy Mother's grace and gentle heart,*
> *And when to Manhood's hopes and duties grown,*
> *Be thou a prop to thy great Sponsor's throne.*

Lady Bessborough, wildly irritated, scribbled hurriedly:

> *May he who wrote ye verse impart*
> *To the sweet Baby whom he blesses*
> *As shrewd a head, a better heart,*
> *And talents he alone possesses.*

Sheridan had to read out the reply, and, having glanced it through, gave himself a moment's grace by pretending that the writing was indistinct, and then read it aloud, rendering the last lines as:

> *A wiser head, as pure a heart,*
> *And greater wealth than he possesses,*

thus scoring heavily on the evening.

But the brilliant concourse who ushered the baby into the social scene could do him no good with all their wishes and prognostications; the evil fairy had appeared, long before the christening-party, and made the gifts of all the good fairies of no avail. Augustus Lamb seemed to have been favoured with precisely those gifts that mere bad fortune can never take away. His father was of vigorous stock, a man of acute and singularly stable intelligence; his mother came of a family not only brilliant, but combining those qualities of intellect and practical ability which had made them statesmen and administrators for centuries; he was the child of a marriage of affection, and both his parents were under thirty at the time when he was born. Few children could have had a better heritage, a more promising start in life.

And yet if the child could have understood, as he gazed languidly at his mother as she hung over him, her ardent face wistful and puzzled as she wondered why he was sleepier than other children, and listened to the people who said that he was too big for his age, he would have seen in that adoring mother a being who had done him an injury in giving him life at all. The common judgment on her that she brought her troubles on herself by wanton irresponsibility, that her vagaries, which made confusion of so much that was valuable and noble, were the result of cold-blooded selfishness, is refuted by the ominous testimony of this birth. The boy grew up with his father's good looks, and with a mind so hopelessly enfeebled that he never attained beyond the capacity of a child of seven.

CHAPTER FIVE

The deficiency was not alarmingly apparent while the child was still a baby, and physically he gave no cause for disquiet; he was well and beautiful. When the commotion of illness and of the christening-party was over, and Augustus installed in a nursery at the very summit of Melbourne House, a new phase of existence was before his mother, and new distractions appeared to fill it. Even had she been more fitted to look after a child than she was, the nursery of an establishment such as Melbourne House cannot be so much the mother's province as it may in smaller houses; and at twenty-two she was still in the first freshness of enjoyment. But now she took her pleasures rather differently; she would still have liked polishing a spar, only she had no opportunity; that capacity for intense, if short-lived, preoccupation with objective interests was now exercised on more adult amusements. She did not break in horses now, though she rode constantly, and got about on horseback when most ladies would have used the carriage. She still drew; indeed, she kept her interest in drawing till the end of her life; and in the diary in Lord Desborough's possession is a charming sketch of William Lamb reading the newspaper, with his legs over the back of the sofa. But "those principles . . . that horror of vice . . . of anything the least improper," these attractive but *gauche* traits of character had been filed away by a skilful hand; and what was left was radiant, animated, ineradicably honest, but without enough scruples to be tiresome. The agitation of early married life, and the illness of childbirth, were recovered from, and, the glaze of that almost childlike innocence and inexperience thawed by the contacts of the world, she was prepared to enter upon the scene with abandonment. In 1810 she began a flirtation with Sir Godfrey Wedderburn Webster, known to fame chiefly through the exploits of his wives; one of whom was divorced and married Lord Holland; the other was enshrined in the poem "Love at Head Quarters," in which her liaison with the Duke of Wellington while in Brussels is vividly described, and for which the editor of the *St. James's Gazette* was sentenced for libel before the House of Lords. Sir Godfrey was a good-natured but stupid man, and it is difficult to

43

believe that Lady Caroline could have taken him with any seriousness. However, the affair was productive of two interesting letters. Sir Godfrey had given her a bracelet and a little dog; his attentions and Caroline's acceptance of them began to alarm Lady Melbourne; it was important, from the point of view of the elder members of that limited society, that liaisons should be conducted with discretion, and that licence should be regulated by common sense. A person who began the game without first having grasped the rules was a menace to all the other players. But Lady Melbourne, though outraged in what might almost be termed the professional instincts of a *grande dame*, may be credited with a more human feeling; though she had not the affection of a wife to keep her faithful to her husband, she yet felt the indignation of a mother when her son was slighted by his wife's preoccupation with another man. She expostulated with Lady Caroline, who was most concerned, but continued to behave just as before. Lady Melbourne began to see at last that the ethereal young lady of the upper floor, with her childlike vivacity and her pale yellow curls, was a match even for Lady Melbourne's heavy artillery. Lady Caroline had not only the waywardness of a spoilt girl; she had, before it had been broken down, and except where her heart was concerned, that supreme indifference to criticism with which her heredity had armed her, and against which the stern, the vigorous, the impressive Lady Melbourne battled in vain. The contradiction of her nature was that she combined a sense, an appreciation of personality so profound that it overrode all conventions, and made it natural to her to ride on the box if she wanted to talk to the coachman, with a complete obliviousness of the collective personality of society, or the significance of anyone's position, apart from his or her interest as a character. With such a disposition, Lady Melbourne might have been expected to accomplish something by throwing aside all forms and meeting her opponent as man to man; but the final touch of exasperation lay in the fact that Lady Caroline was not only a nuisance, and a charmer, and a blue stocking, and a surprise-packet, and a very indecorous young lady; she was also, in the phrase of *La Belle Assemblée*, a first-rate, born in that eyrie that dallies with the wind and scorns the sun. She could, when she wished to protect herself, assume that elusive, impalpable air of detachment that put her quite out of reach and made her politeness a galling insult. Lady Melbourne had had the Duchess of Devonshire in her pocket; she had lorded it over the warm, sweet-natured Lady Bessborough; and it could not have occurred to her at the time of the marriage that the girl would prove any more difficult than the mother and the aunt. But her rebukes and admonitions, though received with the slightly lisping cajoleries, the caresses, the "dear, dearest Lady Melbournes," went off the Ponsonby surface like water from a duck's back. It was distinctly a point to Lady Caroline that she broke up the majestic unpleasantness of The Thorn into honest anger. The *affaire* Webster continued its course, regardless of all the latter might do, until she finally despatched the following note upstairs.

"I only write you a few lines for the purpose of preventing you coming to me loaded with falsehood and flattery, and under the impression that it will have any effects, which I most solemnly assure you it will not. I see you have no shame, no compunction for your past conduct. As I can do no good I shall withdraw myself, and suffer no more vexation upon your account. Your behaviour last night was so disgraceful in its appearance and so disgusting from its motives that it is quite impossible it should ever be effaced from my mind. When anyone braves the opinion of the world, sooner or later they will feel the consequences of it, and though at first people may have excused your forming friendships with those who are censured for their conduct, from your youth and inexperience, yet when they see you continuing to single them out and overlooking all the decencies imposed by society, they will look upon you as belonging to the same class. Had you been sincere in your promises of amendment, or wished to make any return to William for his kindness, you would have discarded and driven from your presence any persons or things which could remind you of the unworthy object for whose sake you had run such risks and exposed yourself so much. But on the contrary you seem to delight in everything that recalls him to you [had she worn the bracelet too often?] and to nourish and foster those disgraceful feelings which have caused so much embarrassment to those who ought to be dearest to you . . . only one word more—let me alone! I will have no more conversation with you upon this hateful subject. I repeat it, let me alone, and do not drive me to explain the motives of the cold civility that will from henceforward pass between us."

But circumstances played into Lady Melbourne's hands. The dog, Sir Godfrey's present, bit Augustus, and the feelings of the anxious mother, which are as compact of imagination as those of the lunatic, the lover, and the poet, worked so powerfully in Lady Caroline, leading her to imagine what her feelings would have been had the dog been mad, and her child sacrificed to her own selfish amusement, that she capitulated completely, but, in writing a submissive letter to Lady Melbourne, she ended with a very significant passage on William Lamb:

"Some heads may bear perfect happiness and perfect liberty, mine cannot, and the principles with which I came to William merited praise and ought to have been cherished; they were the safeguards to a character like mine, and nobody can tell the almost childlike innocence and inexperience I had preserved till then. All at once this was thrown off, and William himself all unconscious of what he had done, William himself taught me to disregard all the forms and restraints I had laid so much stress on. With his excellent heart, sight, head, and superior mind, he might and will go on with safety without them—he is superior to those passions and vanities which mislead weaker characters, and which, however I may be ashamed to own it, are continually misleading me. He called me prudish—said I was strait-laced,—amused himself with instructing me in things, I need never have heard or known, and the disgust I at first felt for the world's wickedness I till then had never heard of, in a very short time gave way to a general laxity of principles which, little by little, unperceived of you all, has been undermining the few virtues I ever possessed."

The importance of this letter, is the fact that it was written in 1810, nearly two years before Lady Caroline ever set eyes on Byron.

Sir Godfrey faded from view, but the Devonshire House cousins, now Lady Georgiana Morpeth and Lady Harriet Leveson-Gower, took up the task and continued to criticise with the animosity they had felt towards Caroline in early youth. *Glenarvon* is dealt with in a later chapter, but as its chief interest is that of a *roman à clef*, it is tempting to quote a passage here and there in connection with the original. The following, if not entirely just as a judgment of Georgiana and Harriet, is of first-rate interest as giving their cousin's opinion of them. The Misses Seymour were the most highly educated young ladies imaginable, and, whenever they encountered opinions differing from their own, it was only to feel a languid surprise that anyone could be so misguided as to entertain them. "To them, the follies and frailties of others carried no excuse with them, and every course which they themselves did not adopt, was assuredly erroneous." The pretty little snap and glitter of these sentences is by no means impersonal. Lady Harriet wrote to her sister in the same year:

"Lady Oxford and Caroline William have been engaged in a correspondence, the subject, whether learning Greek purifies or enflames the passions. Caro seems to have more faith in theory than in practice, to judge at least by those she consults as to these nice points of morality!" The friendly intercourse and exchange of ideas between the two ladies was to be rudely sundered two years later, for this was Byron's Lady Oxford, who resembled "a landscape by Claude Lorrain, with a setting sun: her beauties enhanced by the knowledge that they were shedding their last dying beams," and from whose house he was to write the famous letter published in *Glenarvon*.

The round of visiting went on; to and from Brocket, to Panshanger, where the inimical sister-in-law was no doubt outwardly pleasant, to Melbourne, the Derbyshire estate whose name the Lambs had adopted as their title; in town, besides many smaller establishments such as the Dowager Lady Cork's, there were, as usual, Devonshire House, Carlton House, familiarly known under the Prince of Wales's auspices as "Nero's Hotel," and last, but not least, Holland House, with the notorious but well-nigh incredible Lady Holland.

Lady Holland's natural pungency had been exaggerated by the fact that when, as the divorced wife of Sir Godfrey Webster, she married the co-respondent, Lord Holland, she was not received in London Society. Her house was the meeting-place of almost every man of note, but, even so late as 1841, Sydney Smith had to warn Lord Denman that Lady Holland would be at a party, so that the latter could use his discretion about bringing Lady Denman. As the daughter of a wealthy American planter, Lady Holland had a new-world vigour and independence which was equal to the ease and inconsequence of the highly born English ladies, yet, terrifying as she appeared in her invincible rudeness, and her almost awe-inspiring lack of taste, she did not invariably command the respect which a stupider but more amiable woman would have received in her own house. Sydney Smith, when told to ring the bell, asked if he shouldn't sweep the floor. Count d'Orsay grew tired of picking up her fan, and suggested, at his third or fourth descent, that he should spend the rest of the meal under the table;

while William Lamb, on being ordered to move his seat at dinner, exclaimed, "I'll be damned if I dine with you at all," and walked out of the room. Nevertheless, Holland House was one of the *salons* of the century, though it was said that its chief attraction was not Lady Holland, with her sky-rocketing tactics, but the charming nature of Lord Holland. Ladies whose position was such that they made their own rules visited there, including naturally, Lady Caroline Lamb, who left a satirical account of the *ménage* in *Glenarvon*, into which she was provoked by Lady Holland's outspoken criticisms of her, after a period of intimacy which left Lady Caroline unprepared for the sudden change of attitude.

An account of two morning visits, one to Lady Oxford, "Lady Mandeville," and one from Lady Cahir, who had first introduced Sheridan to Devonshire House, and who appears as Lady Augusta Selwyn, has an authentic ring. Lady Caroline who calls herself Lady Avondale, with the Christian name of Calantha, found Lady Mandeville reclining upon a sofa. A shawl was thrown gracefully over her, and her hair in dark auburn ringlets, half concealing her languishing blue eyes. " 'I am glad you are come, my loved friend,' she said, extending her hand, 'I have just finished translating an Ode of Pindar:—his poetry is sublime —it nerves the soul and raises it above vulgar cares:—but you do not understand Greek, do you? Indeed to you it would be a superfluous acquisition, married as you are to such a man.' Lady Avondale rather puzzled as to the connection between domestic happiness and the Greek language, listened for further explanation; but with a deep sigh her lovely acquaintance talked of her fate, and referred to scenes and times long passed and utterly unknown to her. She talked much too of injured innocence, the malignity of the world, of her contempt for her own sex, and of the superiority of men, and the entrance of three gentlemen, whom Lady Mandeville introduced as her lovers, gave a new turn to the conversation; and here it should be explained that the term lover, when Lady Mandeville used it, was intended to convey no other idea than that of an humble attendant, a bearer of shawls, a writer of Sonnets and a caller of carriages ... the conversation alternately touched upon the nature of love, the use and beauty of the Greek language, the pleasures of maternal affection, and the insipidity of English society. Lady Avondale had been used however to a manner rather more refined, more highly polished than any she found out of her own circle and family." When Lady Avondale returned from Lady Mandeville she found Lady Selwyn alighting at the door. " 'Ah, my dear, sweet friend,' she cried, flying at Calantha and shaking her painfully by the hand, 'this fortuitous concurrence of atoms fills my soul with rapture ... Why were you not at the ball last night? ... it was monstrously dull ... unsupportable, I assure you, perfectly so. Mrs. Turner and her nine daughters. It is quite a public calamity, Mrs. Turner being so very prolific—the produce so frightful ... what is the matter? you look so *triste* to-day, even my wit can't enliven you. ... Now I have it; you have perchance been translating an Ode of Pindar. I was there myself this morning, and it gave me the vapours for ten minutes; but I am used to these things, you know, child, and you are a novice. ... But you are freezing, *mon enfant*, what can be the matter? I will release you in a moment from my visitation. I have ten thousand things to say. Will you come to my opera box next Tuesday? Are you going to the masked ball on Thursday? ... Oh, by the bye, why were you not at your aunt Lady Margaret's concert? I believe it was a concert—there was a melancholy noise in one of the rooms, but I did not attend to it. ... Farewell—*adieu*, remember to-night—bring Lord Avondale, that divine Henry, though beware, too. Many a lady has to mourn the loss of a husband as soon as she has introduced him into the society of *fascinating* friends.' 'He is out of town.' 'Then so much the better. After all, a wife is only pleasant when her husband is out of the way. She must either be in love or out of love with him—If the latter they wrangle, if the former it is ten times worse.' ... 'Which are you, in love or out of love with Mr. Selwyn?' 'Neither, my child, neither. He never molests me, never intrudes his dear dull personage on my society. He is the best of his race and only married me out of pure benevolence. We were fourteen raw Scotch girls, all hideous and no chance of being got rid of, either by marriage, or death, so ugly and healthy. I believe we are all alive and flourishing somewhere or other now. Think then of dear, good Mr. Selwyn, who took me for his mate because I let him play cards whenever he pleased. He is so fond of cheating, he never can get anyone but me to play with him. Farewell, *au revoir*—I shall expect you at ten. *Adieu, chère petite*.' "

In *Glenarvon*, at the point at which these visits were taking place, the divine Henry was represented as becoming estranged from his wife, from his inability to check her extravagance or control her moods;

and, in real life, William Lamb was also showing signs of dissatisfaction. In 1809 there was a disappointment, a child was still-born, and in this year he had made the famous entry in his commonplace book: "The general reason against marriage is this, that two minds, however congenial they may be, or however submissive the one may be to the other, can never act like one. Before I was married, whenever I saw the children and the dogs allowed, or, rather, encouraged to be troublesome in a family, I used to lay it all to the fault of the master of it, who might at once put a stop to it if he pleased. Since I have married, I find that this was a very rash and premature judgment."

With regard to dogs, however, Lady Caroline does not seem to have been unamenable. She wrote from Brocket:

"Plunger ran away from me yesterday, and Francis found him parading at the top of the park with some stray poultry. I would not bring my pretty Phyllis, as you wished not." And then comes to the part which she had perhaps been postponing:

"I think lately, my dearest William, we have been very troublesome to each other; which I take by wholesale to my own account and mean to correct, leaving you in retail a few little sins which I know you will correct." "Condemn me not to silence," she asks, a pathetic plea, reminding one of George Lamb's retort when she asked him what was the eighth commandment, and was told, "Thou shalt not bother." "Assist my imperfect memory," she continues: to the extent perhaps of reminding her of the date when she wrote her letters; she had headed her congratulatory note on Lady Maria Fane's engagement, "Brocket, Heaven knows what day." "I will on the other hand be silent of a morning, entertaining after dinner, docile, fearless as a heroine in the last volume of her troubles, strong as a mountain tiger . . . you should say to me, Raisonnez mieux, et repliquez moins." The disagreements were smoothed over: who could have resisted so candid and endearing a confession? They went to the Isle of Wight for a holiday with Augustus, and Lady Sara Spencer, the daughter of Lady Bessborough's brother, describes their arrival:

"William, Caroline and Augustus Lamb arrived here next door to us yesterday. They are quite well, and as yet very well pleased with us and Ryde, but as they have been living almost a London life at Cowes with the Duke of Gloucester, dinners, balls and evening parties in succession, I expect they will find us uncommonly dull before long."

William Lamb fulfilled this prophecy: at least, he left his family and returned to London shortly afterwards. Lady Caroline sent him as wifely a letter as anyone could desire:

"I have been playing all day with that pretty little Augustus of yours. He is the dearest child I ever saw, and shows where you are gone by pointing to the sea."

CHAPTER SIX

It is an ungracious task to vilify Byron, to whom everyone who is fond of poetry owes a debt of gratitude, and who had so much in his character that is more interesting to dwell on than his faults. But a slight survey of his less estimable traits is almost necessary to explain his connection with Lady Caroline Lamb.

It is no slight to Lady Caroline to say that in reality she was the last person to attract, far less to hold, the affection of Byron. Scattered through his works are images of the female character he admired. Haidée, passionate and gentle, simple and loving, is perhaps the most beautifully drawn. He had almost completely the Oriental conception of feminine charm, as well as of feminine limitations; and Lady Caroline Lamb conformed to neither. His scornful pronouncement that a woman needed nothing but a mirror and a box of sweets to keep her happy could not be applied to her; and he told Medwin therefore that she had no heart, but made up for the deficiency in head; and, though her appearance caused so much sensation among ordinary people, it was of all kinds of attractiveness the most foreign to his taste. He told Lady Blessington:

"Sentimentalists may despise buxom health and rosy hue, which has something dairy-maid like, I confess, in the sound; but I have the association of plumpness, rosy hue, good spirits and good humour all brought before me in the homely phrase, and all these united give me a better idea of beauty than lanky languor, sicklied o'er with the pale cast of thought, and bad health and bad humour, which are synonymous . . . a delicate woman, however prettily it may sound, harrows my feeling, with a host of shadowy ills to come, of vapours, hysterics, nerves, megrims, intermitting fever, and all the ills that wait upon weak women, who, when sickly, are generally weak in more senses than one." Lady Caroline might have escaped the charge of languor, but she was undoubtedly slender. "Her figure, though genteel, was too thin, wanting that roundness that grace and elegance would vainly supply." Not only was her figure incorrect, but her temperament was uncongenial to a degree; that bold and independent attitude, that obliviousness of propriety, contrasting so oddly with her fragility, was the antithesis of what Byron liked in a woman. It is often noticed that the more unrestrained in his own indulgences a man may be, the more rigid are his ideas of female behaviour; and it is therefore not surprising that,

A heart whose love is innocent,

though admired by everybody, should have been especially admired by Byron. Even so, one cannot but be somewhat surprised when he says, "For the general good, I think that all women who had forfeited their reputation should lose their places in society." As this maxim was delivered to Lady Blessington in Italy, it was perhaps formulated while he reposed on the bosom of the Countess Guiccioli.

What was it, then, which accounted for the attraction which kept him for nine months "an almost constant inmate" of Melbourne House? Apart from the fact that so unusual a degree of charm would have some degree of attraction even for a man not ordinarily susceptible in that direction, Lady Caroline was an object of genuine admiration to Byron; she represented social success, friendship, ease, consequence: and at a time when he was in the uncomfortable state of knowing himself to be a genius, but of not being known by other people as such; conscious of his noble birth, but not of an ability to impress others with it. A liaison with Lady Caroline Lamb was gratifying to every feeling of exasperated self-importance; and though, on the publication of *Childe Harold*, everyone was dying to know him and Lady Caroline was at least as anxious for his acquaintance as he could be for hers, yet he had somehow to make his *entrée*, and, once he were within the Devonshire House circle, he had no more fields to conquer. Lady Blessington, although she knew him when he had known the soothing and ameliorating influence of praise and admiration, the fullest recognition, gave it as her opinion that he was morbidly sensitive to consideration of worldly importance.

"If he sometimes forgets his rank, he never can forgive anyone else's doing so, and as he is not naturally dignified, and his propensity to flippancy renders him still less so, he often finds himself in a false position by endeavouring to recover lost ground!" The adoration, spontaneous and unstinted, of Lady Caroline was very sweet; the *entrée* of Carlton House, Melbourne House, Devonshire House, perhaps even more gratifying. Byron was as much taken with pomp and

53

circumstance as any parvenu, and hardly more discreet in his enthusiasm. "I should say," said Lady Blessington, "that a bad and vulgar taste predominated in all Byron's equipment, whether in dress or furniture. I saw his bed at Genoa when I passed through in 1826, and it certainly was the most gaudily vulgar thing I ever saw . . . his carriage and his liveries were in the same bad taste, having an affectation of finery, but *mesquin* in details and tawdry in the *ensemble*, and it was evident that he piqued himself on them by the complacency with which they were referred to. He even asked us if they were not rich and handsome, and then remarked that no wonder they were so, as they cost him a great deal of money. At such moments it was difficult to remember that one was speaking to the author of *Childe Harold*."

But though sufficient reason for his temporary devotion could be discovered in her name, her house, her friends, there were, despite the grave incompatibility, traits in her which delighted him until they were over mastered by others he abhorred. She told Medwin, 'my only charm in his eyes was that I was innocent and enthusiastic,' and Byron made a remark to Lady Melbourne which accounts for all and any of his affairs. "I would love anything that seemed to ask for it . . . my heart always alights on the nearest perch."

Their meeting occurred at Lady Jersey's ball. Lady Caroline had been lent *Childe Harold* by the sea-green and impeccable Mr. Rogers; and declared that she must meet the author. Rogers said:

"He has a club foot and he bites his nails."

"If he is as ugly as Æsop, I must see him," she answered. But when she actually saw him, the centre of an admiring circle of women who were "throwing up their heads at him," as she described it, she turned away without permitting an introduction. The famous words were written in her diary the same night: "Mad, bad and dangerous to know," and much of the voluminous body of Byron biography has hardly improved on them.

A few days later she was riding in the country round Kensington, and stopped at Holland House on her way back.

"I was sitting with Lord and Lady Holland when he was announced; Lady Holland said, 'I must present Lord Byron to you.' Lord Byron said, 'That offer was made to you before; may I ask why you rejected it?' He begged permission to come and see me. He did so next day. Rogers and Moore were standing by me; I was on the sofa. I had just

54

come in from riding, I was filthy and heated. When Lord Byron was announced I flew out of the room to wash myself. When I returned Rogers said, 'Lord Byron, you are a happy man. Lady Caroline has been sitting here in all her dirt with us, but as soon as you were announced she flew to beautify herself.' Lord Byron wished to come at 8 o'clock when I was alone; that was my dinner hour. I said he might."

The next day he called, and was shown Augustus. The dissolute man who yet loves children redeems his character, and Byron's great fondness for them is surely one of his most endearing traits. He sat for "hours" with the child in his arms, not moving for fear of waking him. Lady Caroline's own eagerness in showing him her baby no doubt pleased him.

Nevertheless, even at this stage of the acquaintance, he appeared to discover more fine-ladyism and oddity than was pleasing. Three days afterwards he brought her a rose and a carnation (in 1824 she had them still); he gave them to her with the sardonic comment, "Your ladyship, I am told, likes all that is new and rare, for a moment." She wrote in reply a letter which, though queerly formal, betrays her in its very stiffness, so foreign to the easy style in which she ordinarily wrote:

"The rose Lord Byron gave to Lady Caroline Lamb died in despite of every effort made to save it; probably from regret at its fallen fortunes. Hume at least who is no great believer in most things, says that many more die of broken hearts than is supposed. When Lady Caroline Lamb returns from Brocket Hall, she will despatch 'The Cabinet Maker' to Lord Byron, with the flower she most of all wishes to resemble, as, however deficient its beauty and even use, it has a noble and aspiring mind, and having once beheld in its full lustre the bright and unclouded sun, that for one moment condescended to shine upon it, never while it exists could it think any lower object worthy of its worship and admiration. Yet the sunflower was punished for its temerity, but its fate is more to be envied than that of many less proud flowers. It is still permitted to gaze, though at the humblest distance, on him who is superior to every other, and though in this cold and foggy atmosphere it meets no doubt with many disappointments, and though it never could, never will, have reason to boast of any peculiar mark of condescension or attention from the bright star to whom it pays constant homage, yet to behold it sometimes, to see it gazed at, to hear it admired, will repay all. She hopes therefore when brought by

55

the little page it will be graciously received, without any more taunts and cuts about Love of what is new.

"Lady Caroline does not plead guilty to this most unkind charge, at least no further than is laudable; for that which is rare and distinguished and singular ought to be more prized and sought after than what is commonplace and disagreeable. How can the other accusation of being easily pleased, agree with this? The very circumstance of seeking out that which is of high value shows at least a mind not readily satisfied. But to attempt excuses for faults would be impossible with Lady Caroline. They have so long been rooted in a soil suited to their growth that a far less penetrating eye than Lord Byron's might perceive them, even on the shortest acquaintance. There is not one, however, that shall not instantly be got rid of, if Lord Byron thinks it worth while to name them. The reproof and abuse of some, however severe and just, may be valued more than the easily gained encomiums of the rest of the world.

"Miss Mercer, were she here, would join with Lady Caroline in a last request during their absence, that besides not forgetting his new acquaintances, he would eat and drink like an Englishman till their return. [Byron's stringent dieting methods, under which he took nothing but potatoes, rice, vinegar, captain's biscuits, and soda water seem to have shocked her.] The lines upon the only dog ever loved by Lord Byron are beautiful. What wrong then that having such a proof of faith and friendship in this animal, Lord Byron should censure the whole race by the following unjust remarks:

> *Perchance my dog will whine in vain*
> *Till fed by stranger hand*
> *But long ere I come back again,*
> *He'd tear me where I stand.*

March 27th, 1812. Good Friday."

This letter cannot but presage how badly the affair was going to turn out; it is not only much too long, but so much too outspoken in its devotion. Not that simple and candid avowals were disagreeable to Byron, but in these circumstances his rigid sense of conventionality must have been shocked, even if he were at the same time flattered, by such remarks as those about the sunflower. It is curious to notice, artificial as the tone of it is, how very much it is the letter of someone in love; the writer cannot resist the pleasure of copying out the verse, although it was known to the reader better than to herself; and already Byron's influence had subdued her: the transformation was not a success, but she was for the moment denuded of her own personality and re-created on the lines of one of Byron's tender, subservient heroines, without any sense of humour. The letter in the original must have had an additional charm, written in the firm but delicate, long-shaped hand, on her paper with its three blue cockle-shells and sapphire-blue edge. At all events, Byron was sincerely taken with her, to judge from his own letter at the time and his subsequent remark to Lady Melbourne —"My attachment *was*, and is not."

For some weeks, while she had the charm of novelty, her ebullitions of wildness were borne with. Dallas gives the following discreet but suggestive narrative:

"One morning he was so absorbed in the composition of a letter to her that he barely noticed me as I entered the room. I said 'Pray go on,' and sat down at one side of the table at which he was writing, where I looked over a newspaper for some time. Finding that he did not conclude, I looked at him, and was astonished at the complete abstraction of his mind,—at the emanation of his sentiments on his countenance. He had a peculiar smile on his lips, his eyes beamed the pleasure he felt at what was passing from his imagination to his paper; he looked at me and then at his writing, but I am persuaded he did not see me, and that the thoughts with which he teemed prevented his discerning anything about him. I said—'I see you are deeply engaged.' His ear was as little open to sound as his eye to vision. I got up; on which he said 'Pray sit.' I answered that I would return. This roused him a little, and he said, 'I wish you would.' I do not think he knew what passed, or observed my quitting him. This scene gave me great pain; I began to fear that his fame would be dearly bought.

"I called on him next day, when I found him in his usual good humour. He told me to whom he had been writing, and said he hoped I never thought him rude. While I was with him, the Lady's page brought him a new letter. He was a fair-faced, delicate boy of thirteen or fourteen years old, *whom one might have taken for the lady herself*. He was dressed in a scarlet hussar jacket, and pantaloons trimmed in front

57

in much the same manner with silver buttons and twisted silver lace, with which the narrow slit cuffs of his jacket were also embroidered. *He had light hair curling about his face,* and held a feathered hat in his hand which completed the scenic effect of this urchin Pandarus. I could not but suspect at the time that it was a disguise. If so he never disclosed it to me, and as he had hitherto had no reserves with me, the thought vanished with the object of it; and I do not precisely recollect the mode of his exit. I wished it otherwise, but wishing was in vain."

Dallas gives an account of Lady Caroline's first connection with Byron; which, if true, has been suppressed by her in the description quoted already, though it is not altogether incompatible with it. According to Dallas, Byron received, immediately on the publication of *Childe Harold*, a copy of verses with a letter beginning "Dear Child Harold," expressing the greatest admiration, and advising him to be happy. "Neither the letter nor the verses was badly written, and the lady concludes with assuring him that though she should be glad to be acquainted with him, she can feel no other emotion for him than admiration and regard, as her heart is already engaged to another." "Byron," said Dallas, "determined at first not to answer this; but on finding his correspondent to be a fine young woman distinguished for eccentric notions, he became so enraptured, so intoxicated, that his time, his thoughts, were almost entirely devoted to answering [her letters]." Eccentric notions, whenever they occur in the description of an anonymous lady, are taken as a matter of course to refer to Lady Caroline Lamb, and this passage seems to tally with the other; describing Byron's absorption in their early correspondence, of which Dallas claimed to have been an eye-witness.

Lady Caroline told Medwin that at the time of her meeting with Byron: "I was the happiest and gayest of human beings, I do believe, without exception." One of the favourite amusements was dancing; the waltz, which was said to have made its appearance after the Battle of Austerlitz, was the rage of the moment, and one would imagine Lady Caroline to have danced beautifully, even if we had not the testimony of the *Morning Post* that she was "a correct and animated waltzer." Her enthusiasm for dancing was unbounded. "At Melbourne House . . . Waltzes and Quadrilles were being daily practised; Lady Jersey, Lady Cowper, the Duke of Devonshire (i.e. 'Hart') Miss Milbanke, and a number of foreigners coming to learn. You may imagine what forty or fifty people dancing from twelve in the morning till near dinner time, all young, gay and noisy, were. In the evening we either had opposition suppers, or went to Balls and routs." The forty or fifty people cannot *all* have been noisy if one of them was Miss Milbanke; as Lady Melbourne's niece Annabella was naturally a visitor of Lady Caroline, and it was at this time that she described her in various uncharitable nicknames—"Fair foolishness," "Beautiful silliness" and said that she seemed clever at anything that was not within the province of common sense, and that she ba-a-ad like a little sheep. But Miss Milbanke was not the only carping visitor. Byron's inability to dance himself made him dislike the amusement for other people, and possibly was at the bottom of his ferocious attack on waltzing in particular:—

> But ye, who never felt a single thought
> For what our Morals are to be, or ought;
> Who wisely wish the charms you view to reap,
> Say, would you make those beauties quite so cheap?
> Hot from the hands promiscuously applied
> Round the slight waist, or down the glowing side;
> Where were the rapture then to clasp the form
> From this lewd grasp and lawless contact warm?
> At once Love's most endearing thought resign,
> To press the hand, so pressed by none but thine,
> To gaze, upon that eye which never met
> Another's ardent look without regret;
> Approach the lip which all, without restraint,
> Come near enough, if not to touch, to taint;
> If such thou lovest, love her then no more,
> Or give, like her, caresses to a score,
> Her mind with these is gone, and with it go
> The little left behind it to bestow.

And his influence cleared the apartments of Comus's rout; the morning waltzing parties were given up; Lady Caroline promised him she would never waltz again, and they shut themselves up together. "My only charm . . . was that I was innocent, affectionate and enthusiastic . . . I was not a woman of the world. Had I been one of that sort, why should he have devoted nine whole months almost entirely to my society? have written perhaps ten times a day, and lastly have pressed me to leave all and go with him. . . . He was then very good, to what he afterwards grew, and his health being delicate, he liked to read with me and stay with me out of the crowd." If anyone doubts that he wrote ten times in one day, there is evidence that at this time he gave her a book a day. In Lord Desborough's library at Panshanger are three books, given, as the inscriptions on the fly-leaves show, to her on three consecutive days. The following letter, the earliest as given in the *Letters and Journals*, is, of those we have, perhaps the most instinct with real feeling; and describes the nature of the charm he felt:

Undated.

"I never supposed you artful; we are all selfish—nature did that for us. But even when you attempt deceit occasionally, you cannot maintain it, which is all the better; want of success will end the tendency. Every word you utter, every line you write, proves you either to be sincere or a fool. Now as I know you are not the one I must believe you the other.

"I never knew a woman with greater or more pleasing talents, *general*, as in a woman they should be, something of everything, and too much of nothing. But these are unfortunately coupled with a total want of common conduct. For instance, the note to your page—do you suppose I delivered it? Or did you mean that I should? I did not, of course.

"Then, your heart, my poor Caro! What a little volcano! that pours lava through your veins, and yet I cannot wish it a bit colder, to make a marble slab of as you sometimes see (to understand my foolish metaphor) brought in tables, vases, etc., from Vesuvius when hardened after eruption. To drop my destestable tropes and figures, you know I have always thought you the cleverest, most agreeable, absurd, amiable, perplexing, dangerous, fascinating little being that lives now or ought to have lived 2,000 years ago. I won't talk to you of beauty—I am no judge. But our beauties cease to be so when near you, and therefore you have either some, or something better. And now Caro, this nonsense is the first and last compliment (if it be such) I ever paid you. You have often reproached me as wanting in that respect, but others will make up the deficiency. Come to Lord Grey's. At least, do not let me keep you away. All that you so often *say*, I *feel*. Can more be said,

60

or felt? This same prudence is tiresome enough, but one *must* maintain it, or what *can* one do to be saved? Keep to it."

This is a good letter, but one regrets not having any of those which made him, as he wrote, oblivious to sight and sound, his eye "beaming with pleasure" as he transferred his ideas to paper. Here he had already reached the admonitory stage; he enjoined prudence, but he did not know of whom he asked it. Lady Caroline said that during the nine months of their intimacy people asked them to parties together, as if they had been married; that this was the result of her behaviour and not Byron's is clear. The second Duchess of Devonshire, in telling Augustus Foster of the situation between Miss Milbanke and Byron, says "your little Friend Caro William as usual is doing all sorts of imprudent things for him and with him." A little later in May there was some idea that Byron was off to Greece. "He is going back to Naxos, and then the husbands may sleep in peace. I should not be surprised if Caro William were to go with him; she is so wild and imprudent."

Rogers enlarges the point; he was more shocked than Lady Elizabeth. He said, "She absolutely besieged him. He showed me the first letter he received from her in which she assured him that if he was in want of money, all her jewels were at his service." This seems to be quite a different letter from what Dallas describes as the first; and therefore it is worth mentioning that her own explanation, in *Glenarvon*, of the fact that she had offered Byron her jewels, was that he had made her so many presents that she felt obliged to give him something precious in return. *Glenarvon* alone is no very valuable testimony as to what actually happened, but it may perhaps be considered where Dallas and Rogers contradict each other. Rogers goes on to say: "They frequently had quarrels, and more than once on coming home I have found Lady Caroline walking in the garden [of Rogers's house in St. James's Place] and waiting for me to beg that I would reconcile them. When she met Byron at a party she would always, if possible, return home from it in *his* carriage and accompanied by *him*; I recollect particularly their returning to town together from Holland House. But such was the insanity of her passion for Byron that sometimes when not invited to a party where he was to be, she would wait for him in the street, till it was over! One night after a great party at Devonshire House to which

Lady Caroline had not been invited, I saw her, yes, saw her, talking to Byron with half of her body thrust into the carriage into which he had just entered.

"In spite of all this absurdity, my firm belief is that there was nothing criminal between them."

Rogers's last remark is an odd one, and suggests that if he, as an eye-witness, could hold such an opinion on this point, his opinion on other matters may not be very trustworthy. Here he is not only proved to be wrong, but he seems to have been alone in his delusion. Apart from gossip and scandal, the matter is settled by the following letter of Lady Caroline's, written to Byron, given as undated in the *Letters and Journals*:

"You have been very generous and kind *if* you have not betrayed me, and I *do not think you have*. My remaining in town and seeing you is sacrificing the last chance I have left. I expose myself to every eye, to every observation. You think me weak and selfish, you think I do not struggle to withstand my own feelings; but indeed it is exacting more than human nature can bear, and when I came out last night, which was of itself an effort, and when I heard your name announced, the moment after I heard nothing more, but seemed in a dream . . . I felt so ill I could not have struggled longer. Lady Cahir said 'You are ill; shall we go away?' which I was very glad to accept. But we could not get through and so I fear it caused you pain to see me intrude again . . . I have been drawing you Madame de Staël as the last I sent was not like. If you do not approve this, give it to Murray; and pray do not be angry with me.

"Do not marry yet, or if you do, let me know it first. I shall not suffer, if she you choose be worthy of you, but she will never love you as I did. I am going to the Chapel Royal at St. James's. Do you ever go there? It begins at half past five and lasts till six; it is the most beautiful singing I ever heard; the choristers sing 'By the Waters of Babylon.' The Peers sit below, the women quite apart. But for the evening service very few go, I wonder more do not—it is really most beautiful for those who like that style of music. If you never heard it, go there some day, but not when it is as cold as this!

"How very pale you are—What a contrast with Moore! 'Mai io l'ho veduto piu bello che ieri, ma è la beltà della morte,'[1] or a statue of

[1] I never saw him more beautiful than yesterday, but it is the beauty of death.

white marble, so colourless, and the dark brow and hair such a contrast. I never see you without wishing to cry. If any painter could paint me that face as it is, I would give anything I possess on earth:—no one has yet given the countenance and complexion as it is. I only could if I knew how to draw and paint because one must feel it to give it the real expression."

Passion has a strange influence; who would suppose this letter to have been written by a "wild, odd, delicate" being, a Faerie Queen? The warmth and tenderness that is afraid of his venturing out on so cold a day, although she was doing so herself, merges into an almost marmoreal solemnity. "I never see you without wishing to cry. If any painter could paint me that face as it is, I would give anything I possess on earth." The passage in which we recognise her is that which describes her as overpowered by her feelings at the sight of him where she could not speak, and yet she was struggling against the weakness of her nerves and her will; it was "more than human nature could bear," but she tried to leave so as not to irritate him by a scene of illness, and, when the crowd made it impossible, her only thought was that her reappearance would annoy him. But she could only persevere in these attempts so long as she felt her influence with him, and that was not to be for long. The reaction, inevitable in the case of two such natures, had already begun in Byron; he was tired of talkativeness, of restless vivacity, of being made conspicuous; her mind gave him no repose; her person was too thin; he was not really unkind, but he was bored and exasperated and leaned more and more towards the idea of marrying Miss Milbanke, who was quiet, serious, and chaste. "I am easily governed by women, and she gained an ascendency over me that I could not easily shake off. I submitted to the thraldom long, for I am indolent and hate scenes, but I was forced to snap the knot rather rudely at last . . . even during our intimacy I was not at all constant to the fair one, and she suspected as much. In order to detect my intrigues, she watched me and earthed a lady into my lodgings, and came herself, terrier like, in the disguise of a carman. My valet who did not see through the masquerade, let her in, where to the despair of Fletcher, she put off the man, and put on the woman. Time 9 in the even. It was worthy of Faublas!"

Though Lady Caroline had tried to be unselfish while she felt that she was beloved, the perception that she was losing his affection drove her quite beside herself; while the relationship was in that distracting condition in which coldness was still relieved by small returns of kindness, she was goaded out of all common sense into trying to revive the happiness of a few weeks ago, so near at hand still that it could not be quite gone. What William Lamb was saying and thinking at this period is not known, but Lady Bessborough was beginning to be alarmed. She had, according to Byron, been mainly responsible for his pursuit of Lady Caroline in the first place, by assuring him, in trying to avert the situation, that he was not beloved, but only encouraged to pique another admirer; Byron no doubt laid more of the responsibility at her door than could be justified, but it must be admitted that she was not the woman to handle the affair; she was too emotional, feeling too deeply and lacking the necessary strength to lay down an uncompromising course, keep to it, and compel her daughter to do the same. Hobhouse notes two interviews he had with Lady Bessborough, and, though he gives hardly any particulars of them, particulars seem unnecessary.

"*June 30*. Came home and found a very odd note from Lady Bessborough.

"*July 2*. Called on Lady Bessborough; a very curious scene.

"*July 3*. Received a note from Lady Bessborough. Went to Byron, who agrees to go out of town.

"*July 6*. Arrived in London. Found on my table strange letters from Melbourne House.

"*July 16*. Walked, by desire, to Lady Bessborough's in Cavendish Square, in the midst of our conversation in comes Lady Caroline Lamb, who talked of Lady Bessborough, and myself looking guilty. Here's a pass for the world to come to!"

One may imagine Lady Caroline, nervous and defiant even with her mother, a prey to growing anxiety, her nerves and temper becoming more and more out of control.

On the morning of August 12th, Lord Granville Leveson-Gower received a letter from Lady Bessborough:

"Oh G! Caroline is gone! It is too horrible. She is not with Byron, but where she is, God knows!" On the same evening a longer letter followed:

"Oh G, I have suffered terribly to-day, but she is found. I have obtained of William and the Melbournes to try her once more and for the

64

present all is quiet again, therefore pray do not mention her flight to anyone, and if you hear of it, for it is but too possible, I fear, explain that it was *unaccompanied*, unknown to anyone. But I will try to tell you what happened. I was at Whitehall in the morning, trying to persuade Caro to come with me to Roe, and let William join us on the Friday to go to Ireland. She was in a bad humour, and in the midst Lord M. came in and reproached her for some of the strange things she does. She answered so rudely, so disrespectfully, that I was frightened, and ran to call Lady Mel. We returned instantly together, but met Lord M. on the stairs, pale as death, screaming to the porter to stop Caroline. It was in vain; she had disappeared in a moment, too quick for the servants who ran after her to guess which way she had turned. I cannot tell you my agony, yet I believed for a long time what Lady Melbourne thought probable, that after the first impulse of anger was over, she would return. I drove up and down Parliament Street in every direction. I thought she could have gone and returned in despair: when Lord M. told us she had threatened him with going to Lord Byron, and he bid her go and be——, but did not think he would take her. On this she ran down. We went, Lady Melbourne and I, immediately there, but found him as much astonished and as much frightened when he heard it as we were. He promised to restore her if she were to be found, and he kept his word. Meanwhile I drove or walked to every place I could think possible she would be. I had promised to dine with Hart. About 9 I went there, quite exhausted, hoping, as he had seen her in the morning, he might give me some idea to find her. I had not been there long, when I received the enclosed from Lord Byron, with a packet of letters she had written and sent to me by the hackney coachman whom she took to carry her away, luckily. She gave the man one for Lord Byron's servant, telling him to inform his master that he would find a note from her in C. Square (the note, like those to us, was taking an entire leave of him). Lord Byron, by following, threatening and bribing the hackney coachman at length prevailed on him to carry him to where she was. He found her at a surgeon's house in Kensington, forced his way in, for she refused to see him or anyone, having told the people that she had run away from her friends, and never would return to them; he passed her for his sister, and brought her away almost by force, to Cavendish Square; where, I am mortified to say, it was more by his persuasions than mine, and almost reproaches at her bearing to see me

65

suffer so much that she was induced to return with me to Whitehall. I went in before her, and William most kindly promised to receive and forgive her. The Melbournes, too, were very good, and she seemed much touched by their reception. But how long will it last? Oh G, what will come of it? I dread to think, and am afraid I shall never get her to go with me to Ireland. I dread too, its being known, for it was noon-day and she ran all up Pall Mall, concealed herself in a chemist's shop till she thought pursuit was over, sold a ring by which she got money to pay the hackney coach. Ordered the man to drive through the first turnpike off the stones; he took her to Kensington, I think of the bad look to the lackeys employed at Holland House. Then she borrowed twenty guineas on a fine opal ring you have seen her wear, and her plan was going to Portsmouth, and embarking in the first vessel that sailed from there, wherever it might happen to be bound for. What an escape! She had taken a place in a stage. G, dear G, all this will end ill, if it does not to her, it will to me. I do feel very unwell; and have for the last hour spit up so much blood that I think some little vessel must have broken. Why is it not a large one? I do no good to anyone, and am grown rather a burden than a pleasure to all those I love most. . . . If I can but get her to go, I do not mind, and will set out to-morrow; but now, though all seems so calm and she promises well, she has declared she believes herself to be breeding; and that the travelling will certainly make her miscarry, and W. is so anxious to have another child that she has nearly persuaded him that it will be best not to go. I know not what to do! I never saw so distressing a creature, and yet when she thought me in danger, almost distracted with grief and remorse, swearing one moment that she will destroy herself if I am ill, and the next that if Lord Byron offers to stir out of London, she will certainly fly— if not *with* him; *from* everyone else. Dear G, I can write on nothing else."

Lady Bessborough's condition had aroused the indignation of her servants, and the housekeeper at Cavendish Square, Mrs. Peterson, sent a letter to Lady Caroline:

"Cruel and unnatural as you have behaved, you surely do not wish to be the Death of your Mother. I am sorry to say you last night nearly succeeded in doing so. She had fallen in a fit at the bottom of her Carriage, and with the utmost difficulty her footmen got her out. O Lady

Caroline, could you have seen her at that moment you surely would have been convinced how wickedly you are going on. She was perfectly senseless and her poor mouth drawn all to one side and as cold as Marble we was all distracted even her footmen cried out *shame* on you for alas you have exposed yourself to all London—you are the talk of every groom and footman about Town. A few months ago it was Sir Godfrey and now another has turned your head and made you forget what a husband you have what an angel child besides making you torture all your kind relations and friends in the most cruel manner. Your poor Father too was heart-broken at seeing the wretched state you had reduced your Mother to—we got Mr. Walker quick as possible and thank God she is better—Lord Bessborough would not let me send for you he said the sight of you would make her worse. You have for many months taken every means in your power to make your mother miserable and you have perfectly succeeded but do not quite kill her— you will one day or other fatally *feel* the wickedness of your present conduct. O Lady Caroline, pray to God for strength of mind and resolution to behave as you ought for this is dreadful.

"J. H. PETERSON.

"I feel by sending you this I offend you for ever but I cannot help it."

We do not know whether Lady Caroline answered the letter, but she accused herself wholly and bitterly to Lord Bessborough.

"MY DEAREST PAPA,—I am but too well aware that I am the cause of my Mama's illness, that my foolish and wrong conduct has caused it; but this idea has given me such a shock that I really require some little time to recover. To shew you that I do not mean to abuse of it, I solemnly promise you to remain in your sight at Roehampton, not to leave you for a day or hour, so that I cannot make any wrong use of the permission. William is very anxious indeed that I should make this short delay of ten days for particular reasons, and I am certain my nerves are so shaken, and I have been so ill these three days, that to hurry off immediately will make me quite so. But I should never have thought of considering myself if Crofts and Sir H. H. had not positively said that it was madness to take Mama on a journey of that sort; far from medical help at such a time. They said, delay it for a month; I only ask ten days, and that my motive may not be suspected, lock me up if you choose during that time, but do not refuse this to your own child, your only daughter, who with all her faults, loves you so dearly.

"I have begged Crofts to explain to you *why* he wishes me not to go independent of my mother and he will call upon you to-night, only wait ten days. . . . If it was for my mother I would cheerfully sacrifice everything, but they sacrifice *her* to *me*. Believe me, dearest papa,

"Your most affectionate and wretched child,

"CAROLINE LAMB."

In a letter written at the same time to Lady Bessborough, she reiterates, with frantic insistence, that she must have a few days of quietness before undertaking the strain and stress of travel. Whether she were merely mistaken or actively deceitful with regard to her being pregnant does not affect the sincerity of her request; she admitted her bad behaviour, she did not want to see Byron again, she was ready to do anything, only she must first have ten days' rest.

"MY OWN DEAREST, KINDEST MAMA,—Be assured of one thing— that I will go with you whatever happens. I have seen Crofts who objects, but that is nothing. Your will, your happiness, is everything, but I have one request. I would not urge it if it could hurt you. Just delay for five days your journey from Roehampton. You do not know the agitation I have gone through, nor what I have suffered. I will not speak of thinking I had lost you. Had it been so I should not have recovered, as it is, my senses are really not straight again. I want a few days to compose me, to get right. Let me go with you to-morrow to Roehampton, but let us remain there a little before we set out. I ask this only because I know and feel that we all want a little repose, and that afterwards, a journey is very well: and now to show you I have no design in all this, I do promise, upon my honour, and soul, that at all events, whether you grant it or not, I will not see Lord Byron. I know Mrs. Peterson and others may think it is an excuse of mine, saying I am with child, but at such a time, would I, could I have the heart to do it? I know also that I have deserved to be suspected, but let me go at all events, only just give me time to recover. You know I said nothing of it, but if it were not so, I wish for a few days quiet. Will you, who are so good, so kind, so generous, you who, though I nearly killed you, I love better than anything on earth, for whose sake I will and have given up what is but too dear to me, will you, my M, ask for this delay? Which, however, if you have set your mind on otherwise, I will not urge. As to letting you go without me, could I? Would you consent? Ah, let us not be parted now. Trust in me at least at this moment; all deceptions are over now; you may see my whole heart if you please.

"Do with me as you will; and only if you think such a request reasonable, grant it!"

It was granted; Lady Bessborough and William Lamb took her to Ireland, arriving at Bessborough on September 7th.

CHAPTER SEVEN

The estate of Kildalton, in Ireland, had been conferred by Cromwell on Sir John Ponsonby for his services, and renamed Bess-Borough by the latter in compliment to his wife Elizabeth. The Marquis of Hartington's castle, Lismore, was not far distant, so a choice of abodes was before the party. If Lady Caroline could have recovered in any circumstances, it would surely have been in the beauty and tranquillity of Ireland, in the society of Lady Bessborough and William, and removed from those scenes of torment. At first, too, it seemed that Byron was kind. She had had, after he had brought her back from her flight, a letter from him; and, though one must mention the suggestion of Miss Colborne Mayne that it may have been a forgery of Lady Caroline's own, like the one by which she obtained possession of the miniature from Murray—written to soothe one hour of her anguish, and kept as a false proof of his affection to show to the world and assist her self-respect—yet, much as there is to be said for this theory, one may also advance the fact that, unlike as the style is to Byron's vigorous and colloquial way of writing, it is not more unlike than might be expected in a letter completely forced and insincere: and Byron was at this time saying to Lady Melbourne, "I must and do write all manner of absurdities to keep her quiet," and secondly, we have Byron's own assertion that, much as he had rather not, he *was* willing, if absolutely called upon, to run away with her and subsequently marry her. He said, "If it is decreed on high, that, like James the fatalist, I *must* be hers, then she shall be *mine* as long as it pleases her, and the circumstances under which she becomes so shall at least make me devote my life to the vain attempt of reconciling her to herself. Wretched as it would render me, she should never know it; the sentence once passed, I could never restore that which she had lost, but all the preparation I could make should be made, and the cup drained to the very dregs by myself so that its bitterness passed from her. In the meantime till it *is* irrevocable, I must and may fairly endeavour to extricate both from a situation which, from our total want of all but selfish consideration, has brought us to the brink of the gulf." The man who could inflict on an innocent wife such a honeymoon as Lady Byron has described, is not likely to have been able to live up to these altruistic promises on behalf of Lady Caroline Lamb. That is not to say, however, that he was not sincere in making them, and is not the letter, written at the very moment of parting, when any lingering feeling, and all instincts of compassion and remorse, would be at their strongest, quite within the bounds of possibility?

"MY DEAREST CAROLINE,—If tears, which you know I am not apt to shed, if the agitation in which I parted from you, agitation which you must have perceived though the *whole* of this most *nervous* affair, did not commence until the moment of leaving you approached—if all I have said and done and am still, but too ready to say and do, have not sufficiently proved what my real feelings are towards you, my Love, I have no other proof to offer. God knows I wish you happy, and when I quit you, or rather when you, from a sense of duty to your husband and your mother, quit me, you shall acknowledge the truth of what I again promise and vow, that no other, in word or deed, shall ever hold the place in my affection which is, and shall be, most sacred to you till I am nothing. I never knew till *that moment* the *madness* of my dearest and most beloved friend; I cannot express myself, this is no time for words, but I shall have a pride, a melancholy pleasure, in suffering what you yourself can scarcely conceive; for you do not know me. I am about to go out, with a heavy heart; because my appearing this evening will stop any absurd story which the event of to-day may give rise to. Do you now think me *cold* and *stern* and *artful*? Will even *others* think so? Will your mother even—that mother to whom we must indeed sacrifice much, more, much more than she shall ever know or imagine? Promise not to love you! Ah, Caroline, it is past promising. But I shall attribute all concessions to the proper motive, and never cease to feel all that you have already witnessed; and more than can ever be known but to my own heart—perhaps to yours. May God protect, forgive and bless you. Ever and ever, more than ever,

"Your most attached,
"BYRON.

"P.S. These taunts which have driven you to this, my dearest Caroline [i.e. Lord Melbourne's saying she might go to Byron, but that he wouldn't take her]—were it not for your Mother and the kindness of your connections is there anything on earth or heaven that would have made me so happy as to have made you mine long ago? And not less *now* than *then*, but *more* than ever at this time. You know I would with pleasure give up all here, and beyond the grave for you, and in refraining from this, must my conduct be misunderstood? I do not care who knows this—what use is made of it; it is to *you* and *you* only, that they are, *yourself*. I was and am yours, freely and most entirely, to obey, to honour, love and fly with you when, where and how you yourself *might* and may determine."

But she must have known really that this was *façon de parler*; she would have been happy if it had not been, as Galt put it, for "the blend of acuteness and frenzy which distinguished her." She had consented to come away because of her mother, but, now that Lady Bessborough was better, she had nothing to distract her from herself, and she knew too well, as she was later to write, that "like the wheels of a watch, the chain of his affection might be said to unwind from the absent in proportion as they twined themselves around the favourite of the moment, and being extreme in all things, he could not sufficiently devote himself to the one without taking from the other all that he had given." Her cousin, Harriet Leveson-Gower, gives a picture of her at this moment.

"The Bessboroughs have been unpacked about a couple of hours. My aunt looks stout and well, but poor Caroline most terribly the contrary. She is worn to the bone, as pale as death and her eyes starting out of her head. She seems indeed in a sad way, alternately in tearing spirits and in tears. I hate her character, her feelings and herself when I am away from her, but she interests me when I am with her, and to see her poor, careworn face is dismal, in spite of reason and speculation upon her extraordinary conduct. She appears to me in a state very little short of insanity, and my aunt says that at times it has been decidedly so."

She adds an illuminating comment on the other member of the party. "My aunt is very gay and amiable. Poor Lord Bessborough *me pèse sur le cœur et l'esprit*. William Lamb laughs and eats like a trooper."

The behaviour of William Lamb is presented in many facets, and it is difficult to divine through them what his attitude of mind may have been. Lady Caroline said, "He was privy to my affair with Lord Byron"

—"When I laugh, play, ride and amuse him, he loves me; in sickness and sorrow he deserts me." Yet she spoke with heartfelt gratitude of his forgiveness. "He was to me what Shore was to Jane Shore;" and, while Harriet Leveson-Gower said he laughed and ate like a trooper, his wife said that he had "that hilarity of mind and heart" that made him welcome in any society. That he was indifferent to her is refuted by his conduct at a time when even a man attached to her would have had reason to withdraw from any active protection of her.

In the meantime, Byron was left in London to prosecute his equivocal friendship with Lady Melbourne undisturbed. His inexhaustible gallantry, at the service of young, middle-aged, and old, had yet another object in The Thorn. It is another instance of how differently the two sexes estimate the same character, and how a woman, notoriously disagreeable to other women, will seem to a man to have just those virtues in which she is most lacking. Byron said to Lady Blessington that what he admired so much in Lady Melbourne was the charity of her disposition, particularly where the failings of other women were concerned. Lady Melbourne was in a strong position; the gentleman who allowed his child to die in a fever-stricken convent, since the only answer he would make to the mother's frantic entreaties to have it removed was "Clare must understand that I cannot have these perpetual scenes," was likely to have the greatest appreciation of Lady Melbourne's tact and *savoir vivre*.

So very reasonable, so unmoved,

with the consummate cleverness that taught her just what failings were disagreeable to a man, and the poise and dignity of an elderly woman that enabled her to keep them always out of sight, she appeared everything that was gracious, solid, piquante, and reposeful; the blend of qualities always agreeable to Byron, and particularly now, as an antidote to the worry of "little Mania." Lady Melbourne's own attitude in the case was exactly in character; the immediate responsibility was removed from her by Lady Caroline's being in Ireland, and in the company of William; she could now enjoy undisturbed the attention of Byron, and, while it would be too much to say that she made the mischief worse, she had so much sympathy for Byron, was so anxious to hear all that he had to say—and it was not a little—of the exasperating "little Medea," that it quite overcame any instinct to be at all tender of

73

her family reputation or her son's honour and feelings. Byron poured himself out in correspondence, and, much as one can sympathise with his irritation, one cannot but be surprised that he should have talked so much about it; any man is annoyed at the persistence of a woman in whom he is no longer interested, but most men wish only to forget the burden, and turn to their friends for distraction. Byron communicated to Lady Melbourne every detail of a frantic woman's delirium; and one is reminded again of how comparatively little, had the telephone been invented earlier, we should have known of the people of the early nineteenth century.

He had already adopted the view that he had never really loved Lady Caroline. "Poor Lady Bessborough! with her hopes and fears. In fact it is no jest for her, or indeed any of us, I must let you into one little secret—*her* folly half did this. At the commencement she piqued that vanity (which it would be the vainest thing in the world to deny) by telling me she was certain I was not beloved . . . this raised a devil between us which I fear will only be laid in the Red Sea." He rejected, with some astuteness, Lady Melbourne's plan of "management." "Manage her! it is impossible, and as to friendship and us—it must be broken off at once, and all I have left is to take some step which will make her hate me effectually, for she must be in extremes." He added in a burst of savagery, "Her worst enemy could not wish her such a fate as *now* to be thrown back upon me." Lady Bessborough's anxiety and distress were viewed by him without sympathy. "It is an odd thing to say, but I am sure Lady B. will be a little provoked if *I* am the first to change . . . and doubtless will expect her daughter to be adored, (like an Irish lease) for a term of 99 years. I say it again, that happy as she must and will be to have it broken off *anyhow*, she will hate me if *I* don't break my heart; now is it not so? Laugh—but answer me truly." Byron's unwillingness to have anything more to do with the affair was intensified by his wanting at the time to marry Miss Milbanke. He hoped that something might happen of itself finally to alienate Lady Caroline before the return of the Bessborough party from Ireland. If not, "you will inform me when they are expected and I will be out of the way unless something occurs to make that unnecessary."

The alternations of tearing spirits and tears, which Harriet Leveson-Gower had noticed, continued—with how destructive an effect may be imagined; but Lady Bessborough writes one cheerful account to Lord

Granville Leveson-Gower. They had removed to the Marquis of Hartington at Lismore.

"Caroline would entertain you with her account of Lismore, which makes Hart furious. She says that when she saw this ruined castle at a distance, she had prepared her mind for every sort of difficulty and adventure—ghosts, knights in armour—that she expected to wind through extensive, though deserted Parks up to the portcullis on the outside, and wander about vast apartments full of tattered furniture and gloom within; instead of which we drove through a dirty village in the middle of which stands the castle without an acre of ground belonging to it. Still she hoped the inside would answer: but that Hart handed her in to, not a Gothic hall, but two small dapper parlours neatly furnished, in the newest Inn fashion, much like a Cit's villa at Highgate, that she cannot recover it and shall break her heart. She also persists in its being very damp. It certainly feels so, though I know not why: for though close to the water it is on a rock. Hart and Caroline had many disputes on the damp, when last night she suddenly opened the door very wide, saying. 'Pray walk in, sir. I have no doubt you are the rightful possessor, and my cousin only an interloper, usurping your usual habitation.' For a long time nothing came, when at last, with great solemnity and many pauses, in hopped a *frog*, Caroline following with two candles, to treat the master of the castle with proper respect, she said." This enchanting picture is solitary; the other gaieties were worldly and enforced, and she wrote letters to Byron about them, partly, perhaps, in a mistaken idea of piquing him, partly in an effort to re-establish her self-respect. It was an error either way, for he seized on it and turned it on her as a weapon. One of his letters to Lady Melbourne gives the substance of his own letter to Lady Caroline.

"Now for C. Your name was never mentioned or hinted at. The passage was nearly as follows:— 'I know from the *best* authority, your *own*, that your time has passed in a very different manner, nor do I object to it, amuse yourself, but leave me *quiet*. What would you have? . . .' and so on, in answer to her description of her *lonely lovelorn condition*!!! much in the same severer style. And now this must end. If she persists, I will leave the country. I shall enter into no explanations, write no epistles, softening or the reverse, nor will I meet her if it can be avoided, and certainly never but in society. The sooner she is apprised of this the better; but with one so totally devoid of all conduct it is difficult to decide." He had now reached the determination of writing no more, and, though he continued to post off to Lady Melbourne the substance of every letter he received, he seems to have adhered to the resolution of writing none himself. On October 20th he announced his departure for Eywood, Lord Oxford's place near Presteign. "I mean (*entre nous*, dear Machiavel) to play off Lady Oxford against her, who would have no objection *perchance*, but she dreads her scenes, and has asked me not to mention that we have met, to C. or that I am going to Eywood."

He was anxious for Lady Caroline to know of his amour with Lady Oxford, but did not wish her to know the actual fact of their being together at Eywood.

"You can make as much use of the incident of our acquaintance as you like with C. only do not say that I am *there*, because she will possibly write, or do some absurd thing in that quarter, which will spoil everything." It is strange to see that, even at this point, Lady Melbourne, whose penetration at least no one denies, was not quite sure that Byron, though exasperated for the present, was really finished with Lady Caroline; that he had previously been writing to her very fully is certain, even though he had recently abandoned it; he has to assure Lady Melbourne: " 'If you mention anything to me' she is sure to have it! How? I have not written these two months but twice. . . . Do not fear about C. even if we meet, but allow me to keep out of the way if I can, merely for peace and quietness. You were never more *groundlessly* alarmed." But how odd that she should have been alarmed at all; in fact, one must suspect that Byron's lack of consistency in round dealing was responsible for the fact that the affair was not definitely finished before. It might have ended in a suicide: his conduct may have been dictated by kindness and an unwillingness to give even necessary pain: but the state of despair alternating with uncertainty and hope was disastrous to her, and a course of magnanimity and kindness which, though he may have laid it out, he was not capable of sustaining, terminated in a burst of long-suppressed anger, and a repudiation more impudently cruel than even Lady Caroline deserved.

What "use" Lady Melbourne made of the information can be conjectured; it did not take Lady Caroline long, on receipt of it, to come to the conclusion that Byron was at Eywood. The awful apprehensions to which this gave rise, the fact that Byron's letters—which had been constant if often disagreeable—had stopped altogether, preyed on her nerves almost to insanity. She wrote and wrote, to Lady Melbourne, to Byron, to Lady Oxford, to Caroline George.

"I have had a tremendous letter from Mrs. George Lamb, who is in a panic about C. . . . Is everyone to be embroiled by C.? Is she mad, or mischievous only? . . . I must presume [her] to be the most contradictory, absurd, selfish and contemptibly wicked of human productions." And, in contrast to this, was the warm languor, the voluptuous tranquillity of Lady Oxford. "I cannot exist without some object of love. I have found one with whom I am perfectly satisfied, and who, as far as I can judge, is no less so with me; our mutual wish is *quiet*, and for this reason I find a double pleasure (after all the ridiculous display of last season) in repose." The lovely peace of Eywood, the beauty of Lady Oxford, illumined by its last rays, mellow as a landscape by Claude—the enjoyment of all this was intolerably disturbed.

> *A wretched soul, bruised with adversity,*
> *We bid be quiet when we hear it cry.*

Byron wrote the letter printed in *Glenarvon*, and therefore as we have it, addressed to Lady Avondale:

"LADY AVONDALE,—I am no longer your lover, and since you oblige me to confess it by this truly unfeminine persecution, learn that I am attached to another, whose name it would of course be dishonourable to mention. I shall ever remember with gratitude the many instances I have received of the predilection you have shown in my favour. I shall ever continue your friend, if your Ladyship will permit me so to style myself. As a first proof of my regard, I offer you this advice, correct your vanity which is ridiculous; exert your absurd caprices upon others; and leave me in peace.

"Your most obedient servant,

"GLENARVON."

She had not heard from him for weeks and then she received a letter in his handwriting; she opened it and found this. It is pointless now to enlarge upon the scene; better to turn to Lady Bessborough, who stands above all the jeers and taunts of Byron and his partisans, a figure great and touching in her absolute devotion to her child. Weak and nervous

77

as she was, no woman could have had less of the heroic temper in her; but when Caroline seized a razor and tried to cut her own throat, her mother grasped the blade, and defied her to pull it through her hand.

They returned to England on November 10th. Lady Caroline was now obsessed with the idea of an interview. "Rational and calm though somewhat plaintive," comments Byron. But Lady Melbourne was anxious no interview should take place, and he promised her it should not. "You will now, I trust, my dear Lady M., think that I have kept to the tenor of our bond; that I have done all in my power to render a renewal impracticable; and I can assure you there are now obstacles in the way sufficient to satisfy Lady Bessborough, if anything could satisfy a personage wavering between Nature and Art: her own fears for the consequences to C. and her anger that so interesting a heroine should not be adored in the oldest and most tedious fashion of feminine worship."

Unhappily, the obstacles did not appear to Lady Caroline to be of so unconquerable a nature that she must turn in upon herself and die or give herself up to the passing of time. We may feel little sympathy with the woman who, married to William Lamb, could be so taken up with Byron; we cannot but condemn the lack of human self-respect, the complete abandonment of all dignity and sense, which her behaviour showed; but the spectacle of agony is not more bearable because we may say that the victim's conduct is insane.

"I found at Cheltenham your letters and C's, and *spared* you the eternal subject by a cessation of ink for three days. I trust this is nearly the last to be shed on the same theme. She charges me with my *own* letters. I have heard that a man in *liquor* was sometimes responsible for what he may have said, and perhaps the same rule extends to *love*; if so, pray make the amplest apology for me. The moment I came to myself I was sorry for it. One thing the lady forgets. For a very long time (in the calendar of Asmodeus,) my answers were the subject of endless reproach on account of their coldness. At last I did write to her without restraint, but rarely without regret. I do not mean to deny my attachment—it *was*—and it is not. It is no great compliment for I could love anything on earth that seemed to wish it."

In the varying fluctuations of feeling between passion, grief, and indignation, she wanted to return and have returned the presents each had made the other. Byron was further exasperated:

'I have some trinkets which she wishes returned, or rather *had*, for God knows where they are by this time. I wish she would not think of returning *mine*, as in that case I must search the country for *hers* ... (they) are travelling (at least most of them) in all parts of England and Wales: they are certainly not in the possession of (Lady Oxford) indeed so anxious was I to get rid of them that most of them had disappeared before my acquaintance with *her*. The truth is they were all women's adornments and looked so out of place in my custody that lest they should seem not honestly come by, I was too glad to find anyone to take them off my hands. . . . She will not deliver up my letters—very well—I *will* deliver up hers nevertheless, and mine she may make the most of."

She was taken down to Brocket, and there, amidst her letter-writing, she found some relief in an extravagant symbolism. She had always been on excellent terms with the villagers of Welwyn, some of whom had been formed into the Welwyn band, who would play at the village festivals she attended, or in the park. Now she assembled some children, who, completely in the dark as to the significance of the scene, docilely followed her instructions as on any previous occasion when she had persuaded them to rehearse for celebrations. The curious performance she devised consisted in burning on a bonfire copies of Byron's letters, and various ornaments, while a troop of village girls dressed in white danced round the flame, and a page recited the following lines which she had composed:

Is this Guy Fawkes you burn in effigy?
Why bring the traitor here? What is Guy Fawkes to me?
Guy Fawkes betrayed his country and his laws,
England revenged the wrong: his was a public cause.
But I have private cause to raise this flame,
Burn also these, and be their fate the same,
Rouge, feathers, flowers, and all those tawdry things,
Beside those pictures, letters, chains and rings,
All made to lure the mind and please the eye
And fill the heart with pride and vanity.
Burn, fire, burn, these glittering toys destroy,
While thus we hail the blaze with throats of joy.

Burn, fire, burn, while wondering boys exclaim,
And gold and trinkets glitter in the flame.
Ah, look not thus on me, so grave, so sad,
Shake not your heads, nor say the lady's mad.
Judge not of others for there is but one
To whom the heart and feelings can be known.
Upon my youthful faults few censures cast,
Look to my future and forgive the past.
London, farewell; vain world, vain life, adieu!
Take the last tears I e'er shall shed for you.
Young tho' I seem, I leave the world for ever,
Never to enter it again; no, never, never!

We know that she read Ford's plays, for she says in *Glenarvon* that she took Calantha's name from *The Broken Heart*, and this scene is worthy of a distraught heroine in Webster or Beaumont and Fletcher. But, though Byron wrote to Lady Melbourne on hearing of it: "Your last anecdote seems to show that our friend is actually possessed by 'the foul fiend Flibbertigibbet, who presides over mopping and mowing,' and if the provincial literati don't insert it in *The St. Albans' Mercury* the collectors of extraordinaries ought to be dismissed for malversation and omission"—yet is it, all things considered, so *very* much more extravagant than some of Byron's own antics at Newstead, where he entertained a group of friends dressed as monks, and made them drink wine out of a skull? But she proceeded to wilder and wilder demonstrations, and her malady, took the form of an intense desire that above all he should know, should realise, what she did and suffered. She had engraved on the buttons of her livery, "Ne crede Byron," and wrote to tell him so. He at once wrote to tell Lady Melbourne; the letters continued, whirling with bewildering rapidity in their vicious circle, and repercussions were beginning to be heard outside it. "Conceive," wrote Byron, "my having heard of it in this wilderness. Lord O. had a lay sermon upon it from his mother and *maiden* sisters yesterday who are all as old as Owen Glendower, and here lived out of the world since Hy. 4th's reign."

Then she perpetrated a piece of really clever audacity.

"January 9, 1813.

"DEAR LADY M.,—C. by her own confession has *forged* a letter in my name (the hand she imitates to perfection) and thus obtained from Mr. Murray in Albemarle Street the picture for which I restored her own. . . . This picture I must have again for several weighty reasons.

"January 10.

". . . Murray is in amaze at the whole transaction and writes in a laughable consternation. I presume she got it by flinging his own best bound folio at his head. I am sure since the days of the Dove in the Ark no animal has had such a time of it as *I*—no rest anywhere. As Dogberry says, 'This is flat burglary.' "

A facsimile of the letter, reproduced in Volume I, of Byron's correspondence with Lady Melbourne, pp. 130–131, and endorsed by Byron —"This letter was forged in my name by Caroline L. for the purpose of obtaining a picture from the hand of Mr. M. January 1813"—is a remarkable piece of forgery, quite indistinguishable from Byron's own writing below. Of the concluding endearments, only "My dearest friend, take care of yourself" are legible beneath Byron's heavy blots and crossings out. He determined to regain the portrait, and both wrote himself and charged Lady Melbourne to do the same. Lady Caroline insisted on an interview, and Byron then changed his mind and thought it better to abandon the whole matter; he said that if such an interview did take place, it must be in the presence of Lady Melbourne, but, if Caroline refused, so much the better. "I did, and do want the picture, but if she will adhere to her present silence I shall not tempt her into further scribbling. You will at least allow I have gained one point. I shall get away without seeing her at all,—no bad thing for the original, whatever may become of the copy." He was journeying between London and Eywood. On April 5th he wrote:

'If in town at all I shall only remain a few days, and it will not be in my power to see Lady Caroline. She has fairly worn out my wish to please or displease her; if she sends you the picture, keep it, but for the love of heaven let me hear no more of or *from* her. . . . I have much to do, and little time to do it in. . . . I give up pictures, letters etc., to her tender mercies; let that satisfy her. The detestation, the utter abhorrence I feel at part of her conduct I will neither shock you

81

with nor trust myself to express. That feeling has become part of my nature; it has poisoned my future existence. I know not whom I may love, but to the latest hour of my life I shall hate that woman."

She continued to urge a meeting, and finally he wrote to her.

"*April 29.*

"If you still persist in your intention of meeting me in opposition to the wishes of your friends, and of mine, it must even be so. I regret it and acquiesce with reluctance. I am not ignorant of the very extraordinary language you have held, not only to me but others, and your avowal of your determination to obtain what you are pleased to call 'revenge,' nor have I now to learn that an incensed woman is a dangerous enemy. Undoubtedly, those against whom we can make no defence, whatever they say or do, must be formidable. Your words and actions lately have been tolerably portentous, and might justify me in avoiding the demanded interview, more especially as I believe you to be fully capable of performing all your menaces, but as I once hazarded everything for you, I will not now shrink *from* you. Perhaps I deserve punishment: if so you are quite as proper a person to inflict it as any other. You say you will 'ruin' me. I thank you, but I have done that for myself already; you say you will 'destroy me,' perhaps you will only save me the trouble. It is useless to reason with you—to repeat what you already know, that I have in reality saved you from utter and impending destruction. Everyone who knows you knows this also, but they do not know—as yet—what you may and I will tell them, as I now tell you, that it is in a great measure owing to this persecution: to the accursed things you have said: to the extravagances you have committed, that I again adopt the resolution of quitting this country. In your assertion you have either belied or betrayed me—take your choice; in your actions you have hurt only yourself, but is that nothing to one who wished you well? . . . You will settle as you please the arrangement of this conference. I once wished, for your own sake, Lady M. to be present, but if you are to fulfil any of your threats in word or deed, we had better be alone.

"Yours, B."

In spite of everything she had done, and of the fact that to the latest hour of his life he should detest her, feeling for her was not quite dead.

Before the "plaguey conference" could occur she was ill, and, though he did not altogether believe the announcement, he said, "If she really is unwell, *all* that Lady C. has done to destroy my regard will not prevent my feeling much regret and sincerely wishing her recovery." When exactly the interview occurred is not easy to determine; her account of it was this: "Lady Melbourne and my mother, seriously alarmed for me, brought me to town and allowed me to see Lord Byron; our meeting was not what he insinuates [in Medwin's *Conversation*]. He asked me to forgive him; he looked sorry for me: he cried; I adored him still, but I felt as passionless as the dead may feel. Would I had died then! I should have died pitied and still loved by him; and with the sympathy of all."

"C. has been quiet to a degree of awful calmness," wrote Byron on June 8th, but it was the lull before yet another storm. It would have been better, perhaps, for her sake, if she had died then; one echoes that one gracious and benevolent sentence of Byron's, "Your actions have hurt only yourself, but is that nothing to one who wished you well?" The famous scene at Lady Heathcote's ball survives in the version of both the actors. Lady Caroline told Medwin that they had continued occasionally to meet: unhappily, she said. Then they met in the middle of Lady Heathcote's ballroom—"he had made me swear I was never to waltz; Lady Heathcote said, 'Come, Lady Caroline, you must begin,'—I bitterly answered, 'Oh yes, I am in a merry humour!' I did so, but whispered to Lord Byron, 'I conclude I may waltz *now*,' and he answered sarcastically 'with everybody in turn—you always did it better than anyone. I shall have pleasure in seeing you'—I did so, you may judge with what feelings. After this and feeling ill, I went into a small room where supper was prepared; Lord Byron and Lady Rancliffe entered after me; seeing me, he said, 'I have been admiring your dexterity.' I clasped a knife, not intending anything. 'Do, my dear,' he said, 'But if you mean to act a Roman's part, mind which way you strike with your knife—be it at your own heart, not mine—you have struck there already.' 'Byron,' I said, and ran away with the knife. I never stabbed myself, it is false. Lady Rancliffe screamed and said I would; people pulled to get it from me; I was terrified, my hand got cut, and the blood came over my gown. I know not what happened after, but this is the very truth."

Byron, according to his own account, knew nothing of the latter part of the scene till told of it by Lady Ossulstone next day. He told Lady Melbourne:

"Since I wrote . . . I have heard a strange story of C.'s scratching herself with glass and I know not what besides; of all this I was ignorant till this evening. What I did or said to provoke her, I know not. I told her it was better to waltz, 'because she danced well, and it would be imputed to *me*, if she did not,'—but I see nothing in this to produce cutting and maiming; besides, before supper I saw her, and though she said, and did even then a foolish thing, I could not suppose her so frantic as to be in earnest. She took hold of my hand as I passed, and pressed it against some sharp instrument, and said, 'I mean to use this.' I answered, 'Against me, I presume?' and passed on with Lady Rancliffe trembling lest Lord Y. or Lady R. should overhear her; though not believing it possible that this was more than one of her, not uncommon, *bravadoes*, for *real feeling* does not disclose its intentions, and always shuns display. I thought little more of this, and leaving the table in search of her would have appeared more particular than proper, though of course had I guessed her to be serious, or had I been conscious of offending I should have done everything to pacify or prevent her. . . . I remained at Lady Heathcote's till five, totally ignorant of all that passed, nor do I now know where this cursed scarification took place, nor when—I mean the room—and the hour. . . . If I am to be haunted with hysterics wherever I go and whatever I do, I think she is not the only person to be pitied. I should have returned to her after her *doorway whisper*, but I could not with any kind of politeness leave Lady Rancliffe to drown herself in wine and water, or be suffocated in a jelly dish, without a spoon or a hand to help her; besides if there was, and I foresaw there would be, something ridiculous, surely I was better absent than present. This is really insanity, and everybody seems inoculated with the same distemper. Lady Westmoreland says, 'You must have done something, you know between people in your situation, a word or a look goes a great way,' etc. etc. So it seems indeed,—but I never knew that *neither* words nor looks—in short downright, innocent, vacant, undefinable *nothing*, had the same precious power of producing this perpetual worry."

Lady Melbourne replied with an account of Lady Caroline's condition, which was certainly difficult enough to tax even the Thorn's powers and resource; but it is dreadful to think of the poor creature, whom nowadays, after such a scene, one would put into a nursing-home for a space of complete rest and quiet, perpetually exacerbated by encounters with Lady Melbourne, well-meaning on the whole as the latter might be.

"She is what she calls calm this morning, and I was in hopes I might have read some parts of your letter to her, and in that intention told her I had heard and that you wish to know how she was, but I soon found that the less I said the better. I asked her if she had any message to send; she said "Tell him I have been ill, that I am now calm, but not very well, but don't tell him what passed the other night." I then said, 'Probably you have told him your own story, have you written?' After an awkward attempt at equivocation she confessed she had but denied your having sent an answer. . . . She then said she should not abuse you; she should keep her thoughts to herself—to the world she should praise your behaviour, and upon my just hinting that she had said shameful things the other night, and that I was glad she had made this determination she went into a rage saying that she would expose you and clear herself, and so on. She is now like a Barrel of Gunpowder, and takes fire with the most trifling spark. She has been in a dreadful—I was interrupted and obliged to put my paper into my drawer and now I cannot for my life recollect what I was going to say—oh, now I have it!—I was stating that she had been in a dreadful humour this last week. With her when the fermentation begins there is no stopping it till it bursts forth, she must have gone to Lady Heathcote's determined to pique you by her waltzing, and when she found that failed, in her passion she wished to expose you, and not feeling how much worse it was for herself. It might have been kept secret but for Lady Oxford and Lady Heathcote, the first from folly, the other from being entirely ignorant of how to be good natured, and from a wish to display her fine feelings. That is the reason why all these women abuse you—how I hate that affectation of sentiment—I knew they would talk, and thought if it reached you it must make you uncomfortable, and therefore desired Lady O. to say to you there had been a scene, but that she was calmed, and I would write to you next morning. At present I am trying to get her out of town, and hope I shall succeed. I was able to send for Frederick [Ponsonby?] whom I knew could hold her, and I could not by myself; and indeed I must do Lady Bessborough the justice to say that her representations of her violence in these paroxysms was not at all exaggerated. I could not have believed it possible for anyone to carry absurdity to such a pitch. I call it so, for I am convinced she knows perfectly what she is about all the time, but she has no idea of controlling her fury. She broke a glass and scratched herself as you call it, with the broken pieces. Lady O. and Lady H. screamed instead of taking it from her, and I had just left off holding her for two minutes —she had a pair of scissors in her hand when I went up, with which she was wounding herself but not deeply. Only if you answer her letters do not let her find out I have written you word of all this. I shall perhaps meet you somewhere; but if I do not, you shall hear how we go on. I cannot describe how frightened I was yesterday.

> "I must finish,
>   "Yrs. ever, E.M."

The scene had certainly made a great sensation; gossip everywhere, and paragraphs in the newspapers. The Duchess of Beaufort wrote from the country to Lady Holland, begging for particulars, because, as she said, "These tales of horror strike me, I assure you, with aggravated terror, in the country, where only imperfect reports reach me . . . you will, I am sure, write and give us every detail"; and Byron wished savagely that Lady Caroline would not call in the aid of so many compassionate countesses.

He had said before, "I know not whom I may love, but to the latest hour of my life I shall hate that woman," and one could not be surprised if these had really been his feelings. But he was not only fickle in his loves; his hates were inconstant too. As the summer progressed, Lady Caroline, perhaps exhausted, perhaps sufficiently recovered to collect herself, actually earned praise on one occasion of Byron's writing to Lady Melbourne: "C. has been a perfect lake, a mirror of quiet, and I have answered her last two letters. I hope they will neither ruffle the lake nor crack the mirror, but when she really and truly has been behaving prettily, I could not write ferociously." He was now entered upon his liaison with Lady Frances Webster, and kept Lady Melbourne informed of all its details. When he was staying with them at Aston, one evening at dinner, Lady Frances directed him to his seat, and as she looked up at him, he told Lady Melbourne, she looked "like C. when gentle."

86

"I am so spoilt by intellectual *drams* that I begin to believe that danger and difficulty render these things more piquant to my taste. As far as the former goes, C. might have suited me very well, but though we may admire drams, nobody is particularly fond of aqua fortis."

And again, "See C.! *if* I should see C.! I hope not, though I am not sure a visit would be so disagreeable as it ought to be."

However, the violent antipathy was easily revived, with the first indication that Lady Caroline was becoming once more restive in her misery. "As for C. we both know her for a foolish, wicked woman, I am sorry to hear that she is still fermenting her weak head and cold heart into an ice cream which will only sicken everyone about her." He had once said that her heart was a volcano. He returned to London, and she called upon him in his rooms in Albany. He was out, and on the table was a copy of *Vathek*, just sent by Murray. She may have turned the pages and lighted upon the description of the Princess Nouronihar and the Caliph Vathek arrived in Hell: "Their hearts immediately took fire, and they at once lost the most precious gift of Heaven, Hope. These unhappy beings recoiled with looks of the most furious distraction. Vathek beheld in Nouronihar nothing but rage and vengeance, nor could she discern aught in him but aversion and despair . . . all severally plunged themselves into the accursed multitude, there to wander in an eternity of unabating anguish. Such was, and such should be, the punishment of unrestrained passions and atrocious actions!" At all events, she chose the fly-leaf of this book on which to leave a message; remembering, no doubt, that brief season when he had given her a book every day, with something written on the first page. She wrote, "Remember me," and left. When he returned and saw the handwriting, he broke out in fury, and wrote beneath:

> *Remember thee: remember thee!*
> *Till Lethe quench life's burning stream*
> *Remorse and shame shall cling to thee*
> *And haunt thee like a feverish dream.*
> *Remember thee! Ay, doubt it not,*
> *Thy husband too shall think of thee,*
> *By neither shalt thou be forgot,*
> *Thou false to him, thou fiend to me!*

CHAPTER EIGHT

Peace was signed between Great Britain and France, and on July 1st, 1814, Wattier's Club gave a masked ball in honour of the Duke of Wellington. Seventeen hundred people were present, including the Duke, who was "in great good humour and not squeezed to death." Hobhouse, in Albanian dress, went with Byron, who—a relic of his early Newstead days—was dressed as a monk. Lady Caroline was also there, dressed as a boy, but masked and dominoed over her male attire. Byron was shocked at this appearance; he was more censorious than Shakespeare would have been. "Not all I could say could prevent her from displaying her green pantaloon every now and then; though I scolded like her grandfather upon these very uncalled for and unnecessary gesticulations." He was now concerned with someone who would no more have behaved in such a manner than would one of his own heroines. In September Miss Milbanke accepted him and, as she was Lady Melbourne's niece, the engagement was yet another topic on which to write daily letters. He enquired of Lady Melbourne whether Caroline had not better be informed. Then he saw a contradiction of the announcement in the *Morning Chronicle*. It must have been her work—"no one else had the motive or the malignity to be so *petty*." But it was not she after all; "I beg her pardon." Moved perhaps with compunction, he went on:

"What is to be done about C.? Ought I to write to her? I am sure no one can be more disposed to pay her every proper attention. If you think it right to say anything on the subject; in short I know not what to do or say, my situation is so difficult with her. To preserve a *medium* is what would be desirable." She apparently wrote him a note of congratulation; thus smoothing the way. He asked Lady Melbourne to say that he would answer it the next day, and added, "I do hope C. will continue in this mood; it becomes her; and it is so provoking to see her throwing away her own happiness by handfuls, when everyone is disposed to forgive and treat her kindly if she would but suffer them." He was married on January 3rd, 1815, and yet there was no sign from Lady Caroline; she did not appear in the bride's bedchamber like

Aspasia, or sit among the Welwyn villagers while they wove the story of Byron's perfidy into a tapestry. On the contrary, she prepared to send a wedding present, but felt a little shy in doing so—Annabella had never liked her, as she knew—so she wrote first to ask whether she might send a gift. Byron told Lady Melbourne. "Bell sent you a few lines yesterday as an accompaniment to an answer of mine to an epistle of Caro's about her present, which of course she will be very glad to receive. I wonder C. should think it necessary to make such a preface; *we* are very well disposed towards her, and can't see why there should not be peace with her as well as with America." In this brief halcyon season he called her "Caro" again.

But, if he were becoming mollified, William Lamb was at last, after so long a period of slumbering, beginning to rise and shake his locks. Byron wanted to know in February, "Is there any foundation for a rumour that has reached me, that *les Agneaux* are about to separate? If it is so, I hope that this time it is only on account of incompatibility of temper, and that no more serious scenes have occurred; in short, I don't know what to wish, but no harm to anybody . . . pray tell me as much as your new code of confidence will permit, or, what is still better, that this report (which came in a letter) is, as the person says it may be, a 'wicked scandal.'" But this was only a premonition, and the wish of some of William's relations, in particular Emily Cowper, was father to the thought. Lady Melbourne answered:

"It may, or may not be, 'wicked scandal,' but as far as I am concerned, it is not true. They are in the country, to all appearance like two turtle Doves. There may be now and then a little sharpness introduced, but who knows that some part of the cooing of these same birds may not be scolding? Really she seems inclined to behave better than she has done, and is only troublesome in private, and a great bore in society. This I know you never *could* believe; but I hope some day to see you undergo a dinner when she wishes to show off."

The year 1815 saw the migration of English Society to Paris after Waterloo, and among the rest the Lambs, who came to the capital via the Low Countries, where they left Lady Bessborough, who had hurried from the south of France to Brussels, where Frederick Ponsonby was lying dangerously ill with wounds received at Waterloo. He had lain out on the field, and been ridden over by a troop of Prussian cavalry.

"Usually," he said, "horses will avoid treading on men, but the field was so covered they had no space to spare for their feet."

Lady Caroline, as usual, captured the general attention; and we have a glimpse of her through the disapproving eye of Fanny Burney, who was in Brussels with her husband. She describes "a large, pleasant party" *chez* Mme de la Tour du Pin, "at which I just missed meeting the famous Lady C—— L——, who had been there at dinner, and whom I saw, however, crossing the Place Royale, from Mme de Tour du Pin's to the Grand Hotel; dressed, or rather *not* dressed, so as to excite universal attention, and authorise every boldness in staring, from the General to the lowest soldier among the military groups constantly parading La Place, for she had one shoulder, half her back and all her throat and neck displayed, as if at the call of some statuary for modelling a heathen goddess. A slight scarf hung over the shoulder, and the rest of the attire was of accordant lightness." Not a toilet to win the approbation of Lord Orville, but how one would wish to have seen this vision, in its ethereal drapery and its short curls, floating across the Place Royale in the dusk.

The boldness thus authorised provided a large circle of admirers; Byron wrote, hoping that she was as happy with the army as he was with Bell. When they came to Paris, Lady Harriet Leveson-Gower was there to mark their arrival with her acidulated pen.

"Nothing is *agissant* but Caroline William, in a purple riding habit, tormenting every one. Poor William hides in one small room, while she assembles lovers and tradespeople in the other. He looks worn to the bone. She arrived dying by her own account, having had French apothecaries in most of the towns through which she passed. She sent them immediately for a doctor, but by mistake they went for the Duke of Wellington." Scott describes a dinner-party with Wellington and Lady Caroline; but these new distractions were suddenly eclipsed by the rumour that Byron was coming to Paris. The Kembles were among the crowd of English visitors, and Fanny Kemble narrates the following episode:

"I remember my mother telling me of my father and herself meeting Mr. and Lady Caroline Lamb at a dinner at Lord Holland's in Paris, when accidentally the expected arrival of Lord Byron was mentioned. Mr. Lamb had just named the next day as the one fixed for their departure, but Lady Caroline immediately announced her intention of prolonging her stay, which created what would be called in French chambers 'sensation.' When the party broke up, my father and mother, who occupied apartments in the same hotel as the Lambs'—Meurices' —were driven into the courtyard, just as Lady Caroline's carriage had drawn up before the staircase leading to her rooms, which were immediately opposite those of my father and mother. A *ruisseau,* or gutter, ran round the courtyard, and intervened between the carriage step and the door of the vestibule, and Mr. Lamb, taking Lady Caroline, as she alighted in his arms, (she had a very pretty, slight, graceful figure) gallantly lifted her over the wet stones; which act of conjugal courtesy elicited admiring approval from my mother, and from my father a growl to the effect—'If you were *my* wife, I'd put your Ladyship *in* the gutter':—justified perhaps, by their observation of what followed. My mother's sitting room faced that of Lady Caroline, and before lights were brought into it, she and my father had the full benefit of a curious scene in the room of their opposite neighbours, who seemed quite unmindful that, their apartment being lighted, and the curtains not drawn, they were, as regarded the opposite wing of the building, a spectacle for gods and men.

"Mr. Lamb, on entering the room, sat down on the sofa, and his wife perched herself on the end of it, with her arm round his neck, which engaging attitude she presently exchanged for a still more persuasive air, by kneeling at his feet, but upon his getting up, the lively lady did so also, and in a moment began flying round the room, seizing and flinging on the floor, cups, saucers, plates—the whole cabaret, vases, candlesticks, etc, her poor husband pursuing and attempting to restrain his mad moiety, in the midst of which extraordinary scene the curtains were abruptly closed, and the domestic drama finished behind them, leaving no doubt, however, in my father and mother's minds, that the question of Lady Caroline's prolonged stay till Lord Byron's arrival in Paris had caused the disturbance they had witnessed."

We need not, perhaps, recapitulate the extraordinary account given by John Mitford in his *Fashionable Follies, Frailties, and Debaucheries,* which comprises a description of Lady Caroline's and Byron's rowing on the lake in the Bois, and subsequently fleeing to Switzerland, hotly pursued by William Lamb, who was ingeniously held up by a broken carriage-wheel and fits of gout: the less so as apparently Byron's projected visit at this time never took place. But the former was very nearly resolved on conquering his indolence, his affection, his inherent scepticism of the usefulness of any marked form of exertion. His brother and sister were passionately anxious to see him separated from his wife, although Lady Melbourne seems to have taken no part in the scheme; and Lady Caroline, on their return from Paris, was playing into her sister-in-law's hands.

On their arrival in England, she was at first prevented from any indiscretions by being laid up with a bad cold. Lady Bessborough had brought back Frederick Ponsonby, whom she was still nursing, and Lord Duncannon was also claiming her attention. She excused herself to Lord Granville Leveson-Gower for not having written, by explaining her circumstances—"Caroline is confined with a cold at Whitehall, Duncannon with inflamation in his eyes in Margaret Street, Frederick with a pain in his side at the top of the house. I, poor soul, *ne sachant me donner la tête*, think of taking another pair of horses as Farquhar does when his patients multiply, and must write flying if I write at all."

But when Lady Caroline recovered, trouble began to assume a nearer and more threatening shape. So far as the outside world was concerned, her behaviour seemed more reasonable. She was now preoccupied with a cause of deep agitation and distress, in that Byron's separation from his wife was imminent. And, as in all her dealings with him, however foolish, selfish, and extravagant they might be, her behaviour was never sordid. She had not seen much of him since his marriage, though one visit had been paid when he and Lady Byron were lodging in Piccadilly.

"Shortly after he married, Lady Melbourne took me to see his wife in Piccadilly: it was a cruel request, but Lord Byron himself made it. . . . Mrs. Leigh, myself, Lady Melbourne, Lady Noel and Lady Byron were in the room. I never looked up. Annabella was very cold to me. Lord Byron came in and seemed agitated—his hand was cold, but he seemed kind." She heard with a mixture of terror and grief that the separation was imminent: for there can be little doubt that Byron had told her of his relations with Augusta Leigh; his confidences were made with the greatest freedom; and it is possible that the extreme virulence of his abuse after the parting from Lady Caroline, during the years of 1813-14, was owing to a suspicion, or a certainty, that she had talked about the affair to other people. At all events, in the final stages of his married life, when by every act of verbal and written indiscretion he was exposing himself to comment, he accused Lady Caroline of having betrayed him. Lady Byron went to her parents in Norfolk on a supposed holiday, and from there he received the intimation from her father that she would not return. The following letters from Lady Caroline to Byron show that Society had got wind of the separation, and that speculation as to its cause was becoming ominous.

"I scarcely dare hope that I shall not offend, however I care not— I must write one line. I must indeed, for I have suffered very, very much —though I cannot presume to hope anything I can say will have any effect, yet do hear those who may advise you better, and whatever may have occurred to occasion a quarrel between yourself and your wife, let no pride or resentment on your part occasion an immediate reconciliation. Go to her—whatever the cause, little or great—it must be made up, nothing can do it but an interview. Lord Byron, you will no doubt be angry at my interfering, where I have no sort of right or interest, but I have witnessed some scenes that I cannot forget, and the agony I suffer at this moment from suspense and alarm is not affected. If you knew what odious reports people circulate when men part from their wives, you would act in this instance prudently—you would not try to irritate Lady Noel or to speak with harshness to Lady Byron, who loves you, would you but conciliate. I know you—fear you, and fear that you will be too offended and too proud to listen to those who would advise you. I have disbelieved all the reports till now: but still I trust they are of far less consequence than some pretend. I care not to know or hear a word about it: but that it is made up, and if you choose to mistake the motive that now prompts me to write this—you may if it please you—it will not alter the truth and I feel it is not a wrong one.

"Could you know what some say, you would really be on your guard. Farewell. Believe me,

"With regret & obediently, Yr. friend & Cousin,

"CAROLINE."

She told him that "amongst those who have most warmly, most zealously supported you against every attack, William Lamb has been the foremost . . . believe me, Lord Byron, we all know you and regard you with attachment and interest that is not to be altered, and though my misconduct and unhappy circumstances have estranged us, you will never find more affectionate relations and friends than in this house. . . . Suppose people tell you anything is known that you think of consequence . . . deny it calmly and to all; do not—do not fancy because every appearance is against you, that it is known. See your wife, and she cannot have the heart to betray you—if she has, she is a devil—and in mercy, be calm."

In her anxiety she joined hands with Lady Melbourne. "Could you know what your aunt suffers, you would write or see her. God bless and preserve you."

As the cloud of suspicion and detraction grew darker, she made a desperate offer—regardless of the fact that it recalled an incident she of all people was anxious to have forgotten.

"Lord Byron, hear me, and for God's sake pause before you rashly believe any report others may make. If letter or report or aught else has been malignantly placed in the hands of your wife to ruin you, I am ready to swear that I did it, for the purpose of deceiving her. There is nothing, however base it may appear, that I would not do to save you or yours from this.

"O Lord Byron, let one who has loved you with a devotion almost profane, find favour so far as to incline you to hear her. . . . Do not drive things to desperate extremes. Do not, even though you may have the power, use it to ill. God bless and soothe you, and preserve you. I cannot see all that I once admired and loved so well ruining himself and others without feeling it deeply. . . .

"Yours, unhappily as it was proved for me,

"CAROLINE."

The situation was past mending, however, the deed of separation signed, and Byron prepared to leave the country. One last effort she made of disinterested friendship. Murray showed her the verses "Fare Thee Well," which he was about to publish, ignorant of what construction might be put upon them by anyone who had an inkling of the real state of affairs; the publisher was not in any case to blame, since, if the lines could hurt anybody, it would be the very man who had given them to him; but Murray did not understand that trait of perverse exhibitionism which was so prominent in Byron's character. Lady Caroline, however, who, as was said, could always be wise for others, though never for herself, saw immediately the folly and the serious risk attending such a performance.

"Judge, Byron, what my feelings must be at Murray's showing me some beautiful verses of yours. I do implore you for God's sake not to publish them. Could I have seen you one moment, I would explain why. I have only time to add that however those about you may make you disbelieve it, you will draw ruin on your own head and hers, if at this moment you show them. I know not from what quarter the report originates: you accused *me*, falsely, but if you could hear all that is said at this moment, you would believe one, who, though your enemy, though for ever alienated from you, though resolved, never more while she lives to see or speak to or forgive you, yet would perhaps die to save you?" Neither of them quite meant what they said about each other in the more violent passages; she was resolved never to see or speak to him again, but they met once more before Byron left England for ever. She saw him in his rooms in Albany. "As he pressed his lips on mine, he said, 'Poor Caro, if everyone hates me, you, I see, will never change—No, not with ill usage,' and I said, 'Yes, I *am* changed, and shall come near you no more.' For then he showed me letters and told me things I cannot repeat, and all my attachment went. It was our parting scene—well I remember it. It had an effect on me not to be conceived—three years I had worshipped him." She did not mean that her attachment went, either. But Byron left the country, and life in Melbourne House became adjusted to a more prosaic scale; the solemn emotions of terror and grief no longer exercised their petrifying weight on nerves and weakness, and, as Byron with his clouds of sulphur disappears, we see again the clear, small details of ordinary life.

The life-story of a successful prostitute is incomplete without one genuine passion which leaves her desolate; and, all things considered, it is fitting that the distinction of planting the fatal dart in the bosom of Harriette Wilson should have been gained by Lady Caroline's cousin, Lord Ponsonby. The story is certainly pathetic—Lord Ponsonby and Miss Wilson had a brief affair of a most romantic nature, in which she at least was passionately in love—"I heard the knock—his footsteps on the stairs, and then that most godlike head uncovered, that countenance so pale, so still, so expressive, the mouth of such perfect loveliness," and so forth. Then, after a few weeks' delirious happiness, a letter containing nothing but a line to say that they must part. George IV had treated Perdita Robinson in the same way. She wandered out into the streets and sat down on a doorstep, unable to say anything except the one word, "Ponsonby"; and after a while a kind old Jew found her and put her into a hackney coach. She never in after life said an unkind word about Lord Ponsonby, but she was naturally not averse from any gossip about his relations. She engaged a French maid who had left Lady Caroline's service, and from whom she gathered the following information:—"Her Ladyship's only son is, I understand, in a very bad state of health and Lady Caroline has therefore hired a stout young doctor to attend on him . . . the poor child being subject to violent attacks in the night, Lady Caroline is often to be found after midnight in the doctor's bedchamber, consulting him about her son. I do not mean you to understand this ironically, as the young Frenchwoman says herself there is very likely nothing in it, although the servants tell a story about a little silk stocking, very like Her Ladyship's, having been found, one morning, quite at the bottom of the doctor's bed. . . . She is always trying to persuade her servants that sleep is unnecessary— being *une affaire d'habitude seulement*. She often called up Thérèse in the middle of the night, and made her listen while she touched the organ in a very masterly style. Her Ladyship's poetry, says Thérèse, is equally good in French, in English or in Italian. I have seen some excellent specimens of her talent for caricatures. She sometimes hires a servant and sends him off next day for the most absurd reasons such as—'Thomas! you look as if you required a dose of salts; and altogether you do not suit me, etc. . . .' She was in the habit of running into her dressing-room to *dédommager* herself with a glass of *eau du vie vieille de cognac*. One day, Thérèse, whose bed-chamber adjoined that of William Lamb, overheard the following conversation between them. *Lady C.* I must and will come into your bed. I am your lawful wife. Why am I to sleep alone? *William.* I'll be hanged if you come into my bed, Caroline, so you may as well go quietly into your own.

"Lady Caroline persevered.

" 'Get along, you little drunken——,' said William Lamb. The gentle Caroline wept at this outrage."

One may take what one likes of this as true, but how very unreliable Harriette Wilson was in her accounts of other people is shown, to give but one instance, in her description of the masked ball at Wattier's, at which she says she had a most interesting conversation with Byron in his monk's habit, and discussed with him his treatment of Lady Caroline, and the portrait of him in *Glenarvon*, two years before the book had been written! It might be argued that Thérèse was more accurate than her mistress, except that she in her turn describes William Lamb as "at all times proud, severe, and altogether disagreeable." The anecdote of the music at midnight is confirmed much later by Bulwer Lytton, and perhaps the conversation with William Lamb is not impossible. The then habit of taking brandy, morphia, ether, and other stimulants and sedatives has often been compared to our own at the present day, and Lady Caroline certainly indulged in it. Harriette Wilson sums up her information by saying that her ladyship must have been very good company, and adds naïvely, "I wish I had the honour of her acquaintance." She added some further details with regard to Lady Caroline's favourite brother, "dearest Willy"; Harriette's sister Amy, another ornament of the profession, had a passionate attachment for William Ponsonby, but, though he frequently attended her theatre suppers, nothing seemed to come of it. At last, however, she told her sisters, "What do you think? Last night William Ponsonby got into my bed." "But," they said, "that is what you have been wanting him to do for the past three months." It appeared, however, that William Ponsonby, in a state of intoxication, had arrived at the house while Amy was out, and, as the servants had orders to admit him at all hours, he went upstairs, and, lying down, proceeded to sleep himself sober. When Amy arrived and entered her bedroom, William Ponsonby pushed his face through the bed-curtains, and, remarking that he wanted sleep, not company, took himself off. This did not diminish Amy's attachment, but it made Harriette very indignant, and "that frightful pale faced William Ponsonby" was held up to much scorn and obloquy in her pages. When this *chronique scandaleuse* was published it came to Lady Caroline's hands, and she scribbled an answer in verse.

> Harriette Wilson, shall I tell thee where,
> Besides my being cleverer,
> We differ? Thou wert hired to hold thy tongue,
> Thou hast no right to do thy lovers wrong.
> But I whom none could buy or gain,
> Who am as proud, girl, as thyself art vain,
> And, like thyself, or sooner like the wind

> *Blow raging; ever free and unconfined.*
> *What should withhold my tongue, with pen of steel*
> *The faults of those who've wronged me to reveal?*
> *Why should I hide men's follies, whilst my own*
> *Blaze like the gas along this talking town?*
> *Is it being bitter, to be too sincere?*
> *Must we adulterate truth, as they do beer?*
> *I'll tell thee why, then! As each has his price,*
> *I have been bought at last—I am not nice,*
> *Kindness and gratitude have chained my tongue,*
> *From henceforth I will do no mortal wrong.*
> *Prate those who please—laugh, censure, who that will,*
> *My mouth is sealed, my thoughts, my pen are still.*
> *In the meantime—we Lambs are seldom civil—*
> *I wish thy book—though not thee—at the Devil!*

However exaggerated the account may be, and undoubtedly is, it certainly indicates that William Lamb was beginning to feel his tolerance unequal to the situation. The last straw was, as one might expect, not an occurrence of grave importance, but one more exasperating scene. Lady Caroline's pages were an accepted part of the entourage of Melbourne House, and the affair arose concerning one of them, who would put squibs into the fire, a habit highly irritating to old Lord Melbourne. Lady Caroline endeavoured to keep the child in order—who knows with what painful if intermitting eagerness? One day in the drawing-room she was playing at ball with him, when the wretched boy put one more of his squibs into the fire. In a passionate burst of irritation and concern, she flung the ball at his head, with such force that it made his temple bleed. He cried out, "O my lady, you've killed me!" "Out of my senses," she said, "I rushed into the hall and screamed 'O God, I have murdered the page!' The servants and people in the street caught the sound, and it was soon spread about. William Lamb would live with me no longer."

Now at last the moment seemed arrived; the mother and sister-in-law had triumphed; William was no longer to endure the vagaries of a wife completely unworthy of his goodness, and they were to separate, although in the interests of decorum the arrangement was to be a purely private one, and Lady Caroline, though dismissed from Melbourne House, was to remain quietly at Brocket. The instrument was drawn up, and the lawyers assembled at Melbourne House. William Lamb was invited to put his name to the document, but first he retired to speak one word to his wife about Augustus, who was to remain with her at Brocket. The company waited for his return, and, after half an hour, George Lamb went upstairs to find him. He discovered him with Lady Caroline sitting on his knee, feeding him with "scraps of transparent bread and butter."

The separation was abandoned; the lawyers might pack up and go home, Lady Cowper and George Lamb retire discomfited. Lady Caroline had, as it happened, behaved in exactly the way to melt his heart. The relations-in-law had congratulated themselves for the past month on her quiet and submissive behaviour. Not a scene, not a protest; she had remained sad and pensive, filled with a sense of misery and of shame. But their rejoicings were premature. If she had burst out once —called in the aid of compassionate countesses or even abused Lady Melbourne—William Lamb's determination would merely have hardened. As it was, she went about, wild and sad, but silent; and, as he watched her, he had time to remember, and to listen to the pleadings of his heart. The strong influence of passionate early love, and the charity of that disposition, "self-indulgent—indulgent to others," overcame the feelings of indignation, and boredom and disgust were charmed away when she sat on his knee and fed him with scraps of bread and butter.

But this new-found serenity was momentarily threatened; almost immediately on the heels of their reconciliation she put into his hands *Glenarvon*. She wrote it, she told Lady Morgan, in one month, while the preparations to separate her from her husband were going forward. "I wrote it unknown to all, (save a governess, Miss Welsh) in the middle of the night. It was necessary to have it copied out. I had heard of a famous copier, an old Mr. Woodhead. I sent to beg he would come to see Lady Caroline Lamb at Melbourne House. I placed Miss Welsh, elegantly dressed, at my harp, and myself at a writing table, dressed in the page's clothes, looking a boy of fourteen. He addressed Miss Welsh as Lady Caroline. She showed him the author. He would not believe that this schoolboy could write such a thing. He came to me again in a few days, and found me in my own clothes. I told him William Ormonde, the young author was dead." The book was published, and the sensation it created was immense. The rag-pickers got to work instantly, and, though the authoress supplied no "key" to the characters, the few principals were easily recognisable, and there were any number of enterprising persons to supply titles for all the rest. Lady Bessborough and William Lamb would undoubtedly have prevailed on her to supress the work had they known about it, but so complete was the secrecy with which she conceived and carried it out that no one knew anything of it until the three small, richly gilt volumes, with their title-page *Glenarvon, or, The Fatal Passion*, and a Love contemplating a burning heart, beneath which is written, "L'on a trop chéri"—were actually on the drawing-room tables.

The chief centre of dismay was Holland House; Creevy, angry and hurt at having been mentioned and his valetudinarianism described, took up the cudgels for Lady Holland, and was sorry to see "Lady Cowper so much depressed and frightened." Lady Holland had indeed received good measure, and one cannot but feel, as one reads those final sentences, forged in the heat of indignation and grief, something of the satisfaction that is felt on seeing a marksman hit the centre of his target. The young Lady Avondale was introduced to Barbary House, where reigned the eccentric Princess of Madagascar, surrounded by a servile mob of reviewers and literary parasites, and supported by the pale poet, known to real life as Mr. Rogers.

"Now who is so ignorant as not to know that this lady resides in an old fashioned Gothic building, called Barbary House, three miles beyond the turnpike? And who is so ignorant as not to be aware that her highness would not have favoured Lady Avondale with an audience had she been otherwise than extremely well with the world?—as the phrase is for she was no patroness of the fallen. . . . At the end of a long gallery, two thick wax tapers rendering darkness visible, the princess was seated. A poet of an emaciated and sallow complexion stood beside her; of him it was affirmed that in apparently the kindest and most engaging manner, he at all times said precisely that which was most unpleasant to the person whom he appeared to praise. This yellow hyena had however a heart noble, magnanimous and generous, and even his friends, could they but escape from his smile and tongue, had no reason to complain."

A conversation ensued between the princess and Calantha, consisting of epigrammatic observations from the former and timid replies from the latter. " 'Is she acting,' said Calantha at length, in a whisper addressing the sallow complexioned poet who stood sneering and simpering behind her chair. 'Is she acting or is this reality?' 'It is the only reality you will ever find in the princess,' returned her friend. 'She acts the Princess of Madagascar from morning till night, and from night till morning.' Calantha then noticed the crowd of reviewers, and asked why they all wore chains and collars round their necks; she was told that such was the fashion at Barbary House, and that no one was tolerated there without the badge of servitude. 'And if I also bow my neck,' said Calantha, 'will she be grateful? May I depend upon her seeming kindness?' The poet's naturally pale complexion turned to a bluish green at this enquiry.

"Cold Princess! where are your boasted professions now? You taught Calantha to love you, by every petty art of which your sex is mistress . . . you laughed at her follies, courted her confidence, flattered her into a belief that you loved her. . . . She fell into the mire; the arrows of your precious crew were shot at her like hissing snakes, hot and sharpened with malice and venomed fire: and you, yes, *you*, were the first to scorn her, you by whom she had stood faithfully and firmly, amidst a host of foes; aye, amidst the fawning rabble who still crowd your door and laugh at and despise you."

It cannot be denied that, with this sort of thing going about, William Lamb's task of rehabilitating his wife in reputation and influence was made more difficult; it was felt that she must show herself at once, the sooner the better, and yet, with so much offended dignity to be met with, the first plunge was painful and hazardous. Lord Granville Leveson-Gower, however, came up to her in public and spoke to her, although his wife Harriet and her sister Georgiana held away. Lady Caroline wrote to thank him afterwards for the very valuable attention, and in the letter throws some light on how the Melbournes had treated her when they thought that William Lamb was going to abandon her.

"My dear Lord Granville,—Thank you for your kindness, but had you not come up, it had been cruel. Do forgive me. I cannot bear that Harriet and yourself should be unrelenting to one who loves you as I do, and who am so near her in blood and affection. You do not know the circumstances, you cannot. Is it to be supposed that after ten years of marriage, and such ill conduct on my part, William would thus support me, at the risk of all he most prizes for himself, if the case were as bad as it is represented? ... Before you judge me, you should see and question the boy to whom I was said to be so barbarous, and whom no offers, no entreaties, can prevail on to leave me. . . . Recollect that at the time I gave this book into the hands of Colburn. . . . I was so miserable that the man himself who spoke with me, did so as if to a person dying. . . . I was ordered out of the house in no gentle language, my Mother was spoke to with the most barbarous roughness in my presence. My husband received letters telling him he would be the public ridicule and jest if he supported me; I was *proved* mad. Mr. Moore assured me I was so, entreated me to persuade my husband of it. I appealed to a few, but my letters were not even answered. I went to Roehampton. Lady Jersey to the exereme annoyance of my Father, quite turned her back on me, and refused to speak to me. I came back to town and met Lord Holland, who coldly passed me by. Indeed, indeed, Lord Granville, I could not stand it. . . . William returned, a dreadful scene passed between me and Lord Melbourne and Mama. That night I sent the book. It was then much more violent. Calantha was not made to die, but it was brought home to real life. William Lamb heard of the novel the day it came out . . . he came in and said 'Caroline, I have stood your friend till now—I even think you ill-used; but if it is true this novel is published, and as they say, against us all, I will never see you more.' . . . You know the rest, but you do not know how William behaved . . . he saw and feels, deeply feels the unpleasant situation that it is for him, but he loves me enough to stand firm as a rock, and to despise such as came forward to ruin one who never hurt them."

She makes a shrewd accusation against Lady Melbourne and Lady Cowper, that "for four years they have supported Lord Byron to the annoyance of William," but now, in their zeal for the latter, they turned on her: "wrongs, crimes, follies, even the last, were raked up from the days of infancy and brought forth to view without mercy. *To write this novel was then my sole comfort.* But before I published it, I thought myself ruined, past recall, and even then I took out all the passages that I thought might reflect on Lady Melbourne and many others." She ends by saying:

"William having once decidedly said, 'I will stand or fall with you,' it was my duty, however painful, to maintain my situation . . . be assured if I did not see how anxious William is about it, for myself I should not care if I retired for ever. Besides you know I am not worldly enough to take measures for what can be purchased any time by a few dinners and balls. It is not therefore from interest that I demand this, but for affection's sake, and because I cannot bear not to see Harriet and Georgiana as formerly. Be not over angry, at my writing this, and believe me, dear Lord Granville, whatever you are to me, ever with respect and affection,

"Yours sincerely,
"CAROLINE LAMB."

It is usual to refer to *Glenarvon* as a book unreadable except that it contains what is meant for a portrait of Byron; and indeed Lady Caroline's faults as a novelist are many; the first, it must be admitted, is that she had no idea of how to write a novel. The story of *Glenarvon* is, roughly, as follows:

The Duke of Altamonte, who owns a large property in Ireland, where the story is laid, has a daughter, Calantha, aged twelve or thirteen when the tale begins, and an infant son, whose mother died at his birth. Castle Delaval is consequently managed by the Duke's sister, Lady Margaret Buchanan, and to a lesser degree by his second sister, Mrs. Seymour. Lady Margaret, a beautiful, ambitious woman, wishes her son, George Buchanan, to succeed to the Altamonte estate, and bribes a young foreigner, named Viviani, to murder the infant by promising to become his mistress when the deed shall be accomplished. Viviani is unable to carry out the scheme for some time, but one morning the baby is found stifled in its cradle; Viviani claims his reward, but Lady Margaret, overcome with horror, repulses him, and he vanishes from the castle. The next portion of the book develops the ingenuous, irresponsible character of Calantha, who at a very early age falls in love with Lord Avondale, a young officer, the nephew of Sir Ralph Mowbray, a peppery Admiral. Lady Margaret is angry at the match, wishing Calantha to marry Buchanan, thus strengthening the latter's prospects of succession; the Duke, to appease his sister and test Avondale's attachment, deprives Calantha of half her dowry and settles it on Buchanan, but Avondale is unmoved—the marriage takes place. A short period of great happiness follows, but soon Calantha's extravagance and wild behaviour, and the suggestions of other people that

Avondale neglects her, cool their fondness, although they have a son and a daughter to whom they are both devoted. Calantha meets the fashionable women of London Society—Lady Oxford in the guise of Lady Mandeville, Lady Cahir as Lady Augusta Selwyn, and Lady Holland as the Princess of Madagascar. The couple return, accompanied by some of these, to Ireland, that Calantha may recuperate in her native air after the fatigues of the season; they find the countryside in an uproar, the Independent Party led by a young stranger, who lays claim to the title and estates of Glenarvon. The peasantry flock to his stronghold, the half-ruined Castle Belfont; two young ladies have run away with him, one of whom, Clara St. Everard, accompanies him dressed as a boy. Avondale is called away to quell the rioters in another district, and Calantha is left at Castle Delaval with unsympathetic friends and tactless relations. A party is made up to visit the ruins of Castle Belfont, and, while the others explore the interior, Calantha prefers to remain outside, alone; attracted by the sounds of a pipe, she walks in their direction, and for the first time sees Glenarvon, leaning against a tree and playing to himself. They are immediately attracted to each other; and, much as the Altamontes disapprove of the rebel party, Glenarvon's fascinations soon make him a welcome guest at Castle Delaval. Mrs. Seymour, the virtuous and gentle aunt, sees with dismay the growing intimacy between Glenarvon and Calantha, but in the continued absence of Avondale it is difficult to check. Meanwhile, after many dark hints have been given out concerning nameless crimes in which Lady Margaret and Glenarvon have been concerned, the former asks Calantha to dismiss her little page, Zerbellini (a child sent from Italy by Viviani to be taken care of at Castle Delaval), because, she says, his fortuitous likeness to the Altamonte family distresses the Duke by reminding him of his son. Calantha refuses to do this, but, when a discussion arises in the family on the impropriety of her giving Glenarvon so many of her jewels, even the pearl necklace that was Avondale's betrothal gift, it comes to light that that particular necklace was not given away, but stolen by Zerbellini, in whose room it is found while he is asleep. Lady Margaret undertakes to have him removed from the castle and kept in good hands at some distance. After many impassioned interviews, Calantha promises to fly with Glenarvon, and is only restrained by the collapse and illness of Mrs. Seymour. Glenarvon takes a tender leave of her and goes to Wales, where Calantha sends him many letters. But her absence, and the presence of the frigid and virtuous but wealthy Miss Monmouth, whom he now decides to marry, weaken Calantha's impression in his heart. At the same time he begins an intrigue with Lady Mandeville, and when a despairing letter, upbraiding him with his silence, arrives, he answers with the famous letter actually sent from Eywood. Calantha is almost crazed with grief, and at this juncture the return of Avondale is announced. An interview takes place in which he states, though without bitterness, his decision to separate from Calantha; he leaves the castle, regardless of her anguish and remorse, and begins a journey to England. Calantha follows him, pursued by the Altamonte servants, but manages to overtake him at an inn, and, worn out with illness and complicated distress, dies in his arms.

Meanwhile Viviani's emissaries have appeared again at Castle Delaval; several intrigues seem on the verge of being unravelled. The Duke is asked to meet a stranger in the chapel of Castle Belfont who will give him welcome news; Viviani has a secret interview with Lady Margaret, who, spirited to the last, defies him, and whom in his fury he stabs to death.

The Duke has now been told that the baby found smothered in the cradle was not his own son, but a peasant baby, stolen and cruelly murdered by one of Viviani's servants; that his real son was spirited away to Italy, and afterwards sent back in the guise of the page, Zerbellini. The child, who was innocent of the theft imputed to him, is now hidden at the Belfont chapel. The Duke hastens to the spot, and on the way discovers his sister's corpse, when he is thrown into hiding by the approach of Viviani, who, unconscious of an ambush, goes to the hiding-place and calls out the child. He asks the boy's forgiveness of all that he has done and is about to do, and then prepares to spring with him over the edge of the cliff, from which feat he is only prevented by the Duke and his retainers. The cloak is plucked from Viviani's face—he is, of course, Glenarvon.

The story ends with the rejoicings at Castle Delaval over the recovery of the heir, and the departure of Glenarvon with a frigate to take part in a naval engagement. Clara St. Everard, whom he had ruined, ties a cloak over her horse's eyes and rides it over a cliff into the sea, while the sky is reddened with the flaming ruins of Castle Belfont.

This story, sufficiently improbable and absurd as it here sounds, is far worse in the original, where it is encumbered with innumerable subsidiary characters—lunatics, patriarchs, simple maidens, all quite unnecessary and very confusing. What is remarkable in the book is that sense of power, misdirected and often overlaid, but occasionally appearing in its true fullness, in a scene, or a description, or even in a reported conversation. But just as Calantha, although "her nature readily bent itself to every art, science and accomplishment, yet never did she attain excellence in any—with an ear the most sensible and accurate she could neither dance nor play, with an eye acute and exact she could not draw, with a spirit that bounded within her from excess of joyous happiness, she was bashful and unsocial in society"—so we are not surprised that Lady Caroline had the gifts of a novelist without being able to write a novel.

Her powers showed themselves in a certain mastery of effect, in the sinister or the passionate. The description is worth quoting of Lady Margaret on the eve of the child's murder, when she had received Viviani's promise, which she would not release him from, and dared not watch to see how he would perform. "She threw up the sash of the window and listened attentively to every distant sound. The moon had risen in silvery brightness above the dark elm trees; it lighted with its beams the deep clear waters of Elle. The wind blew loud at times, and sounded mournfully as it swept through the whispering leaves of the trees, over the dark forest and distant moors. A light appeared for one moment near the wood, and then was lost."

They are apparent too in an occasional sentence that she throws off: "The heart of a libertine is iron; it softens when heated in the fires of lust, but it is cold and hard in itself." And again: "When we love, if that which we love is noble and superior, we contract a resemblance to the object of our passion. . . . Woe be to those who have ever loved Glenarvon!" And once more, in describing the tardy return of Avondale: "Calantha looked upon him as we look afar off, upon some distant scene where we once dwelt and from which we have long departed."

Her description of certain incidents shows that unconscious selection of detail which gives the scenes an importance we cannot analyse, but which we accept. The Altamonte party had attended a concert, which was afterwards followed by dancing, at a house in the neighbourhood, where Glenarvon was present. He followed Calantha to a corner of the room, and said, " 'Give me the rose you wear in return for the one I presented you with in Dunallen Park.' 'Must I?' 'You must,' said he, smiling. With some hesitation she obeyed yet she looked around in hopes no vigilant eye might observe her. She took it from her bosom, and gave it tremblingly into his hands. A large pier glass reflected the scene to the whole company." On another occasion, the same party went on board a warship to dine with the admiral; at their approach the band played a welcome and the occasion was one of joyous mirth, of particular interest to Calantha as she had one of her first serious conversations with Glenarvon. "It was late before the Duke took leave of the Admiral—the guns once more were fired, the band played as for their arrival, but the music now seemed to breathe a sadder strain, for it was heard, softened by distance, and every stroke of the oars rendered the sounds more and more imperfect. The sun was setting and cast its lustre on the waves . . . it was a moment which impressed the heart with awe; it was a scene never to be forgotten."

The chief interest, however, remains in the delineation of the important characters, and in the light which the book throws on small details which are nowhere else preserved. The character of Calantha has, as a self-portrait, considerable merits of detachment while yet preserving some of the charm with which another writer than Lady Caroline herself would have more freely endowed her. She describes herself as a child, silent and shy in the presence of others, but when alone, or carried out of herself, pursuing wildly every impulse of enjoyment, "like a fairy riding upon a sunbeam." Her description of the marriage with Avondale is exceedingly interesting from the biographical point of view, and is a supplement to Lady Bessborough's account of the honeymoon at Brocket.

"Love, like other arts, requires experience, and terror and ignorance on its first approach prevent our feeling it as strongly as at a later period. Passion mingles not with a sensation so pure, so refined, as that which Calantha then conceived, and the excess of a lover's attachment terrified and overpowered the feelings of a child." She describes the first wild excitement of her own life as a young married woman. "She knew not to pause or rest; her eyes were dazzled, her understanding bewildered, and she viewed the world and the new form in which it rose before her with strange and unknown feelings, which she could neither define nor command." The "blend of acuteness and frenzy" mentioned by Galt is nowhere more striking than here, where one may see an account of the wildness and weakness given by the very creature who personified it with the most exact and calm perception:

"Friends! It was the name she was in the habit of giving to the first who happened to please her fancy. This, even, was not required; the favours of the world were sufficient to endear the objects of its censure to her affection, and they who had not a friend and deserved not to have one, were sure to find one in Calantha. All looked fresh, beautiful and new to her eyes, every person she met appeared kind, honourable and sincere, and every party brilliant, for her heart, blest in itself, reflected its own sunshine around. . . . Calantha was esteemed generous, yet indifference for what others valued, and thoughtless profusion, were the only qualities she possessed. It is true that the sufferings of others melted a young and ardent heart into the performance of many actions which would never have occurred to those of a colder and more prudent nature, but was there any self-denial practised, and was not she who bestowed possessed of every luxury and comfort her varying and fanciful caprices could desire? Never did she resist the smallest impulse to temptation. If to give had been a crime, she had committed it, for it gave her pain to refuse, and she knew not how to deprive herself of any gratification. She lavished, therefore, all she had, regardless of every consequence." But the point on which she shows herself remarkable is the delineation of Byron. She had here an unrivalled opportunity to revenge herself for what she undoubtedly felt to be a gross and cruel injury. She had the knowledge; she had the ability; above all, she had the public; and how did she make use of this? Her only attempt at blackening Byron's reputation, apart from ascribing to him murder and kidnapping, to which no one would pay the least attention, and a few incidental seductions, without which the picture would not have been recognisable at all, was to show him overbearing and fickle, faults which everyone knew him to possess, and accepted as part of his remarkable character. When Byron, questioned on the book by Madame de Staël, remarked coolly that the picture could scarcely be like him as he had not "sat long enough," and that the book would have been more interesting if the authoress had confined herself to the truth, he does not seem to have realised how fortunate for himself it was that he was giving his advice too late. In *Glenarvon* he remains, despite exaggeration and absurdity, a dignified and romantic figure. It is characteristic of her that she even ascribes his refusal to dance, not to his lameness, but to interesting melancholy, and the disinclination for thoughtless gaiety of a heart on which the worm was feeding. She said, "To write that novel was my sole comfort," and her sole comfort, even when she hated him, was in dwelling, not on his petty faults, his mortifying disabilities but on his genius and his incomparable charm. There are one or two passages of especial interest, because they carry with them the ring of authenticity. The incident reflected in the pier glass is one, and another, this description of an early encounter: "They were a few minutes alone; he leant over her; she held a book in her hand; he read a few lines, but it is not possible to describe how well he read them. The poetry he read was beautiful as his own, it affected him; he read more, he became animated. *h* Calantha looked up; he fixed his eyes on her; he forgot the poem; his hand touched hers as he replaced the book before her; she drew away her hand, and he took it and put it to his lips!"

Everyone is familiar with the letter despatched under the auspices of Lady Oxford and inserted in *Glenarvon*; what has not been heretofore noticed is another letter, given as from Glenarvon to Calantha after their separation, but before the rupture, and which is almost undoubtedly another genuine letter, so completely is it in Byron's style, and in his most charming style at that, that it deserves a place in his *Letters* at least equal to that of the long letter written to Lady Caroline on her departure for Ireland, whose authenticity has been called in question by Miss Colburne Mayne.

"Were you ever at sea? How does the roar of the mighty winds, the rushing of the water, accord with you? The whistling of the breeze, the sparkling of the waves by night, the rippling of the foam against the sides of that single plank that divides you from eternity? . . . Will you sail? They that go down into the great deep, they see the wonders of the Lord. That thou mayest see as few as possible of His terrific wonders is, my beloved, the prayer of him who liveth alone for thee. The prettiest and most perilous navigation for large ships is the Archipelago. There we will go, and there thou shalt see the brightest of moons shining over the headlands of green Asia, and the isles, upon the bluest of all waves—the most beautiful but the most treacherous . . . dearest, I write folly and nonsense, do I not? But even this, is it not a proof of love?"

For the rest, there is little of outstanding interest. We have no verbatim description of the scene between Lady Caroline and Lord Melbourne, after which she ran out of Melbourne House, so that it is tempting to think that we have an account of it in the incident in which old Sir Ralph Mowbrey attempts to prevent Calantha's escape by locking the door and is foiled by her quickness in escape. A final note of autobiography is discerned in the poem which Calantha composed in her period of misery and disgrace, on the occasion of being blessed by an old man to whom she gave some money.

> *Poor wretch, thou hast nothing to hope for in life*
> *But the mercy of hearts long success has made hard,*
> *No parent hast thou, no fond children, no wife,*
> *Thine age from distress and misfortune to guard.*
> *Yet the trifle I gave, little worth thy possessing,*
> *Has called forth in thee what I cannot repay—*
> *Thou hast asked of thy God for His favour and blessing,*
> *Thou hast prayed for the sinner who never must pray.*

"Long success" had made hard the Devonshire House cousins. Lady Harriet Leveson-Gower went to call, and, entirely oblivious of the nervous strain which Lady Caroline had gone through, and the constant relief and happiness of having averted the separation from William Lamb, she wrote to her sister:

"I went yesterday to Whitehall, and followed the page and Lady Argill through the dark and winding passages and staircases. I was received with rapturous joy, embraces and tremendous spirits. I expected she would have put on an appearance of something, but to do her justice she only displayed a total want of shame and consummate impudence, which, whatever they may be in themselves, are at least better—or rather, less disgusting than pretences or acting a more interesting part. I was dragged to the unresisting William, and dismissed with a repetition of embassades and professions. I looked, as I felt, stupefied, and this is the guilty, broken-hearted Calantha, who could only expiate her crimes with her death. I mean my visit to be annual."

The overpowering relief and pleasure, the pathetic delight and eagerness, at re-establishing once again even a show of family intercourse was frigidly censured by Lady Harriet. "I cannot bear not to see Harriet and Georgiana as formerly"; but Harriet would have thought suicide more decorous, and determined that her grudging visit should be once a year.

But Lady Caroline saw in her, not the cold and unsympathetic Lady Leveson-Gower, but a cousin—a creature that was her idea of what a cousin should be. Well might it be said of her, "She was eloquent, most eloquent, full of ideas, and of graceful, gracious expression. She confounded her dearest friends and direct foes, for her feelings were all impulses, worked on by a powerful imagination."

CHAPTER NINE

In 1816 Benjamin Constant was in London with his manuscript of
Adolphe, of which he was to give a reading to a select few, including
Lady Harriet, who told her sister: "I have begged that Caroline W.
Lamb may be there to cry and make sensation for us." Lady Caroline
had, in fact, more right to be present at a reading of *Adolphe* than her
cousin, for she had been a friend of Madame de Staël while the latter
was in England, and she told Hobhouse that Madame de Staël had
"embraced her very often, and seemed to like it very much." In any
case, her opinion of the work would have been more worth having
than Lady Harriet's. We are grateful to the latter for one piece of
information, however—that Lady Caroline was, among other titles,
nicknamed Cherubina. The name was conferred on her, no doubt,
from her exploits in page's dress after the page Cherubino in *Les
Noces de Figaro*.

The nineteenth century seems to us the era when not only great
writers flourished, but for the first time a profuse undergrowth of
talented but undistinguished authors as well; of these, Sydney Owenson, afterwards Lady Morgan, enjoyed perhaps the greatest amount of
contemporary popularity. She was the daughter of a Shrewsbury trades-
man who removed his family to Dublin and became connected with a
theatrical circle, the members of which encouraged the clever little girl,
who was anticipating Thomas Moore by composing songs and setting
them to traditional Irish tunes.

Her first novel, *The Wild Irish Girl*, brought her fame and money,
and she became friendly with the Duchess of Abercorn, who married
her off, a trifle peremptorily it would seem, to the family physician,
Sir Charles Morgan. Lady Morgan, vigorous and intelligent, good-
natured and adaptable, found it easy to make friends. She came to
London and met Lady Bessborough, who liked her, and Lady Caroline
Lamb, between whom and herself there sprang up a warm friendship;
Lady Morgan was captivated with the grace, talent, sweetness, and
rarity of Lady Caroline Lamb, and something in her own solid yet

cordial personality attracted the fluttering spirit of Lady Caroline as with the force of gravity. The first letter that the latter wrote to her before Lady Morgan's marriage, when they had just become acquainted, was a good introduction to a relationship, for it showed so much, so openly, of Lady Caroline's disposition.

"DEAR MISS OWENSON,—If it had not been near making me cry, what I am going to tell you might make you laugh, but I believe you are too good natured not to sympathise in some manner with my distress. It never occurred to me that I should forget the direction you gave me, so that having ordered the carriage and having passed a restless night, I was but just getting up when it was ready. I ordered it to fetch you, where, was the question—at York, was the only answer I could possibly give, for York, alas is all I remember. Now they say there is a York Lane, three York Streets, a York Place, three York Buildings, and York Court. I knew no number, but immediately thought of sending to Lady Augusta Leith; the Court guide was opened, it was for 1810. Lady A. L. consequently not where she now is, and where either of you are, I cannot think; but as I was obliged to go into the country I wrote this, and take my chance of its ever getting to you.

"See me before you leave town, and send me your number and street, I beg of you; the impression you have made is, I assure you, a little stronger but I never can recollect one direction. Do you think the new man could teach me?

"Yours very sincerely,

"C. LAMB."

"My direction is always Melbourne House."

Lady Morgan's view of her contrasts most welcomely with that of some of Lady Caroline's relations:

"If there is anything more delightful than another, it is the spontaneous outbreak of a good and kind heart, which in serving and giving pleasure to others, obeys the instinctive impulse of a sanguine and genial disposition, waiting for no rule or maxim, not opening an account for value expected, but doing unto others what you wish them to do to you.

"This in one word is Lady Caroline Lamb."

The intimacy was not without its little awkwardnesses, though these were unperceived by Lady Caroline. "The chief cause of the odd things she used to say and do, was that never having lived outside the habits of her own class, yet sometimes mixing with people of inferior rank, notable only for their genius, she constantly applied her own sumptuous habits to them. She called on me one day in London, and struck by my servant who announced her being in livery, she said in her odd manner as she was going downstairs; 'My dear creature, have you really not a groom of the chambers with you? You must let me send you something, you must indeed. You will never get on here with only one servant—you must let me send you one of my pages. I am going to Brocket to watch the sweet trees that are coming out so beautifully, and you shall have a page while I am away.' "

The pages were still a feature of Melbourne House, and rumour, having fed gloriously on the incident of Lady Caroline's throwing a ball at the head of the child who persisted in putting squibs into the fire, was loth to stay empty for long, and manufactured another incident on the model of the last. The dowager Lady Cork was fond of using anybody's eyes that she could to save her own, and one morning, when Lady Morgan called on her, the latter was obliged to sit down and write notes at her dictation. One was to the Duchess of Leeds, recommending a page who was leaving Lady Cork on the ground, said her ladyship, that the household was not sufficiently religious and he was unable to go to church as many times a day as he thought desirable. In order to have two strings to her bow, Lady Cork meant to apply to Lady Caroline as well, which showed a determination to get rid of the boy somehow which hardly suggested that extreme piety was his real drawback. She mentioned a rumour that Lady Caroline had recently broken the head of one of her pages with a teapot; Lady Morgan reminded her that the story was discredited by the fact of Lady Caroline's having been at Brocket at the time the incident was said to have taken place at Melbourne House.

"I don't care whether it's true or not," said Lady Cork. "All pages are better for having their heads broke some time or other. Now please write: Dear Lady Caroline—Will you come to-morrow to my blue party? I send this by that pretty little page whom you admired so, but who, though full of talent and grace, is a little imp whom perhaps *you* may reform, but I cannot. He is very like that boy whom you used to

114

take into your Opera Box with you, and who was so famous for dressing salad." Lady Cork knew Lady Caroline well enough, it seems, to take the right way of recommending the page; it was at her house that Lady Caroline displayed a flash of that spirit that already seemed to belong to the past—a joke reminiscent of Sheridan. A party had been invited to meet Blücher, the subsidiary hero of the day, and every guest had arrived except the lion himself. The occasion was a difficult one; the party hung fire, for everyone was too full of expectation to be entertaining. At last, all hope of his arrival was given up; when suddenly his name was announced on the stairs, the servants were heard cheering, the door flew open, a figure in a cocked hat and greatcoat strode into the room—but the voluminous habiliments contained only Lady Caroline Lamb!

This was a momentary recrudescence of gaiety, but she still pursued her social pleasures. Lady Morgan met her at a party at the Duchess of A.'s; Lady Morgan arrived too early, and found the whole establishment in disorder—footmen running about without their jackets, while a French *femme de chambre* stood directing everybody with her hands in her pockets; Lady Morgan wandered uneasily through the rooms, and says: "I had just drawn near the only fire I met with in the suite when a loud hammering behind me induced me to look back, and there, mounted on a step ladder, stood a bulky elderly lady, in a dimity wrapper and a round eared cap, who was knocking up a garland of laurel over the picture of some great captain of the day . . . as I took the elderly lady for a housekeeper, I asked her if the Duchess were still in her dressing room? No child, said the lady, the Duchess is here, *telle que vous la voyez*, doing what she can get none of her awkward squad to do for her, and down sprang this active lady of seventy, with a deep inspiration of fatigue, ejaculating, 'Gude God, but this pleasure is a toilsome thing!' So saying she bustled off, and in less time than could be imagined, reappeared in the brightest spirits and the brightest diamonds. . . . This party turned out one of the most agreeable I ever was at in my life. I spent the evening seated on the second flight of stairs between Lady Caroline Lamb and 'Monk' Lewis. At two in the morning Lady Caroline Lamb proposed that we should go and sup snugly at Melbourne House, and return to waltz when her Grace's rooms should thin," which they willingly agreed to do.

She was also devoted to opera, and anxious to share her pleasure.

Lady Morgan, during a morning visit to her, had said that *Faust* was said to be wonderful, and that she and Sir Charles meant to hear it if they could. When she got home, she found that a note from Lady Caroline had preceded her:

"Mind the Opera. Come early I beg you, for they say *Faust* is beautiful. I will leave word at the door, it is the private door, near the King's box—ask for me in the Duke of Devonshire's box. . . .Tell Sir Charles I am enchanted with his aunt. I had a great mind to ask her blessing while she was about it—Bless me, even me also. Had I been like her I should have looked upon beauty as a hussy.

"Ever yours,
"C.L."

Sir Charles's aunt then visiting them was an *esprit fort*, who had insisted on a robber being hanged, despite the representation of the neighbourhood that if she persisted in giving evidence she would become dangerously unpopular with certain members of the community. "It amused me," said Lady Morgan, "to see them side by side, the lady of supreme London *ton* and the wealthy old lady *de province*; the contrast between the lisping, soft voice of Lady Caroline, the prim distinct tones of the old lady was curious and amusing." In connection with the opera, another incident, quite characteristic, deserves repeating. She told Murray: "I set out, stark mad in white satin, as Tilburina did, to see Don Juan seized by the Italian, and scarce was my dear fatal name pronounced, Lady Caroline Lamb, when some jocose footman said—Sooner Lady Caroline *Wolf*. At this too just criticism several warm defenders sallied forth among the same precious herd. Whilst they were all fighting, I was very soon kidnapped by 2 rack chairmen, who insisted on carrying me each into his respective chair, I being all the time mainly desirous of getting in and not out of the Opera House. It chanced that I was very fine, having dined out in diamonds and feathers. When I therefore got safe up with a crowd of plumed attendants, my unfortunate dog, that long-cared-for dog, covered with mud like Lord Something's rat, appeared entering the vestibule. At this sight soldiers and servants shouted forth, A Fox! and began hissing it down. Judge of my situation, I was either obliged to give up this dear shabby cur, or own a friend in such a disguise as few had dared to do. The latter was, however, my choice and being much too frightened and late after all these adventures, I turned back to find my carriage almost carried away by Irish boys and drunken chair men, one of whom to the indignation of the rest, constantly vociferated, 'This is my lady'— 'Your lady, d——n you?' 'Yes, my lady'—and sure enough he, like the dog, proved a mendicant pensioner when a blaze of light showed him to me like a ghost."

She still danced, as in the days of the first waltzing-parties at Melbourne House; she had the enviable position of being one of the patronesses of Almack's, the most exclusive of the Regency clubs, and thus possessed the power to give that most coveted benefit, "a ticket for Almack's," to other people. On the occasion of another visit, she offered Lady Morgan a ticket, and told her that if she would send word to Lady Bessborough, the latter would call for her in her carriage. As she entered the room "on the arm of Lady Bessborough," Lady Morgan was in the happy position of being able to nod in a condescending manner to an acquaintance who would have cut her had she been there by herself; Lady Caroline met them at the door, "with a beautifully embroidered sac over her arm." "What have you there?" said Lady Bessborough. "Well, dear Mama, it is a piece of very curious rhubarb, quite like a bon-bon. I brought it to recommend it to Hart; it will do him all the good in the world, he is looking so ill."

But she had more serious diversions. In 1819 George Lamb stood as a candidate in the Westminster election; and Lady Caroline, in her usual eagerness to be of use, and perhaps remembering the exertions of her mother and the Duchess of Devonshire, on behalf of Fox, did not, it is true, repeat their spectacular exploits, but wrote to ask for the support of William Godwin. Godwin refused his vote, but a correspondence sprang up between them, and, as she had felt comfort in the stable temperament of Lady Morgan, she was drawn very much to the support of Godwin's philosophical mind, while he was not slow to discover that she might minister to him. She wrote asking him to visit them at Brocket, saying that she knew a man of his resources would be able to support the dullness of a mere family party. But Godwin did not wish to leave London. When she was at Brocket she wrote to him; and, as ever, she was full of the beauty of the country-side.

"You would not say if you were here that nature had not done her best for us. Everything is looking beautiful, everything in bloom. It is impossible for me to come just yet to London, but I will if I live in June. Yet do not fancy that I am here in rude health, walking about and being notable and bountiful. I am like the wreck of a little boat, for I never come up to the sublime and beautiful—merely a little gay, merry boat, which perhaps stranded itself at Vauxhall or London Bridge; or wounded without killing itself as a butterfly does in a tallow candle. There is nothing marked sentimental or interesting in my career; all I know is that I was happy, well, rich, and surrounded by friends. I have now one faithful kind friend in William Lamb, two more in my father and brother, but health, spirits and all else is gone —gone how? O assuredly not by the visitation of God, but slowly, gradually, by my own fault. You said you would like to see me and speak to me. I shall, if possible, be in town a few days. When I come I will let you know. The last time I was in town, I was on my bed three days, rode out, and came off here on the fourth. God preserve you.

"Yours C.L."

She had written: "The loss of what one adores affects the mind and heart," and when the animation produced by the joy of being forgiven by William Lamb was abated, she began to feel with Samson Agonistes:

Nature in me is weary of herself.

The description of herself given to Godwin is expressed with the truth that distinguished her remarks about herself no less than her shrewd comments on others. From this time onwards she appears in shadow, permanently broken in health; Lady Morgan describes her, too ill or too inanimate to receive visitors except in her bedroom, where the chair in which Byron had sat for his portrait by Sanderson was fastened to the floor in the bow window, and she lay on the bed, "wrapped in fine muslins." The figures which had been so important in her ilfe were one by one departing, and leaving behind them emptiness and shade.

The death of Lady Melbourne in 1818 did not perhaps affect her deeply except in its effect on William Lamb. Byron, in Italy, said:

"The time is past when I could feel for the dead, or I should feel for the death of Lady Melbourne, the best and kindest and ablest female I ever knew, old or young. But I have 'supped full of horrors' and events of this kind leave only a kind of numbness worse than pain—like a violent blow on the elbow or on the head." But in 1821 a worse catastrophe overtook her; Lady Bessborough died while at Florence, where she had gone to nurse Lord Duncannon's son. Nothing remains to mark Lady Caroline's feelings, but the blank is perhaps more impressive than any words. The reader, more than a hundred years after the event, cannot think of it without distress: but the cousins were so hopelessly antipathetic that, though Lady Harriet tried to do the kind thing, she had to say, "Caroline to whom I went with every early feeling of interest and kindness awakened, contrived somehow to deaden both."

With Lady Bessborough dead, Melbourne House empty except for her own apartments, Devonshire House with the second Duchess who could not reinspire the magic gaieties of the first, the last phase of Lady Caroline's existence belongs definitely to that era, gloomy and prosaic, with which we are hopelessly familiar because it ushered in our own. Smoke gradually thickening over London, fields soon to be converted into the wilderness of suburbs, an era for illustration of which one looks to the small, swarming illustrations of Cruikshank, in which the eighteenth-century window-panes are drawn with the cracks and cobwebs of the nineteenth century upon them; the plaster peels in patches off the walls, and the radiant and the simple is hustled out by the press of those squalid, grotesque, sordid, vital figures which fill the commercial, the mechanised, the over-populated—in a word, the modern age. An anonymous writer, contributing to Bentley's *Miscellany* an account of the occasion on which he saw Lady Caroline, begins it by an encounter with Miss Benger on the steps of the British Museum. On a dark and wet afternoon, at the closing of the reading room, he stood waiting to venture out. "Still dripped the rain, and still, for it was four o'clock, out poured the dark contents of the reading room—the melancholy company of hacks, ghostly, unwashed, unshaven creatures, all with greatcoats, I observed, most of them having good umbrellas, their stock in trade, their carriage and horses, the great support of that dim gentility which one might trace amid the havoc of poverty and work . . . work uncheered by companionship, unalleviated by the encouragements of fame." Among the crowd, an elderly lady, in a tippet which he describes as the produce of some consumptive bear, appeared and required the aid of his umbrella. This was Miss Benger, one of the earliest of that group of lady historians of which Agnes Strickland was the chief. Miss Benger and her life of Mary Stewart were well known in their own day, and the anonymous owner of the umbrella was glad enough, when he found out who the lady was, to continue the acquaintance. He said that Miss Benger lived in Doughty Street, where she held literary gatherings and entertained her friends with weak Bohea, innocent finger biscuits and gentle negus, and it was here, he says, "that I met with that singular ill-starred woman, Lady Caroline Lamb." But how changed from "the delicate Ariel," "the fairy riding on a sunbeam." "She was a gentle ladylike little woman with slight remains of comeliness, yet pleasing from the delicacy of her appearance. The neatness and finish of her attire was striking, when all the others seemed to have dressed extempore . . . there was nothing in her aspect of that passion which breathes in every line of *Glenarvon*, that most remarkable and powerful book which passion alone could have dictated. There was none of that impatience and daring self-will to be detected in her passive manner and soft voice, which betrayed her into the madness of stabbing herself for Byron's love. All was ladylike, correct, somewhat uninteresting—perhaps a little sad."

The figure, brilliant under the chandeliers of Devonshire House, is hardly recognisable, sitting quietly amid the obscurity, the gloom and dust of Doughty Street. One livelier episode, however, is recounted by Cyrus Redding. "Lady Caroline Lamb used to link the noble and plebeian together. Then came morning calls, the worst possible things for economical single ladies, had not 'morning' meant between three and four in the afternoon. One day Lady Caroline called on Miss Benger . . . she had with her one of those little dogs, for which I never could conceive the use till this incident occurred. . . . Lady C. and the hostess were sitting side by side on the sofa, deeply immersed in the merits of the last new novel, when the little poodle cur proceeded to extract from beneath the sofa an old slipper, a pair of stockings, a couple of pocket handkerchiefs, and so on to the inexpressible misery of the owner, whose heels were continually exerting themselves *au derrière* as if Lady C.L. were unconscious of their efforts in endeavouring to push back some article of female habiliment, intended for the bag of the washerwoman. Nothing could avail, the room was strewed with the spoils when Lady C. L. rose to depart. O for the feeling of that moment when her Ladyship walked over the stairs—no matter, death has extinguished alike the mortification of the one and the polished regret of the other."

Lady Caroline's interest in the literary circle of Doughty Street, besides being accounted for by her ever-awakening interest in anything that she came across, and her appreciation—doubly felt now—of friendliness and kindness towards herself which she naturally found in full measure among Miss Benger and her associates, was also enhanced by the fact that she had continued her own literary career. She had that indifference to the merit of her own performances which distinguishes the amateur who really understands his subject. She had told Byron that she could produce a better portrait than anyone else could she but draw and paint, and Calantha was described as unable to do either, although possessed of the true eye; yet she had as much skill, at least in pen and ink drawing, as would have made most people think themselves able to draw. Among examples of her work are the drawing of William Lamb in her diary, already mentioned; an irreverent little caricature of Byron and Lady Byron, the stumpiness of whose figure and her regularity in church-going Lady Caroline had once said to be the two greatest objections to the match; a curious picture of the infant Bulwer Lytton, seated on a sea-girt rock, and entitled "Seul sur la Terre," which she made once when his parents brought him to Brocket, many years before his friendship with her began. The musician Nathan, who set to music Byron's Hebrew Melodies, a fact which was no doubt the origin of Lady Caroline's interest in him, has reproduced in his *Fugitive Pieces* a charming and spirited invitation to Miss Love to sing at a concert. He describes its production thus: "I proposed the powerful aid of Miss Love's rich voice. Lady Caroline instantly exclaimed: O do ask her to come; will my writing to her assist you? And immediately seated herself as if to pen the necessary epistle, when instead of a letter to Miss Love, as I expected, I received the following hieroglyphical card, neatly executed—Love—a cupid kneeling on a cloud—implores Love to come to——" Then follow three hastily drawn but excellent little pictures of an ornate chariot, a ring, a dash, and then a lamb, with its curls and black feet. As she had no opinion of her drawings, so she had none of her writing either; she said that her "vital spark" was about as much as a maid could get out of a tinder-box. Nevertheless, she rebelled against the not unnatural anxiety of her connections to prevent her publishing anything further; she reminded herself that she was descended from Spenser, and, what was still more to the purpose when it came to getting one's own way, from the redoubtable Sarah Jennings. She continued to write short poems, some of which appeared in annuals, of which the best have a distinct touch of grace and vigour; Byron told Lady Blessington that C. wrote prettily; and the "Waters of Elle," to which Nathan composed the music, may perhaps represent what was best in her non-autobiographical poetry; when she was on the theme of personal experience she achieved, with less technical merit, a far greater degree of interest.

The Waters of Elle

Waters of Elle, thy limpid streams are flowing
Smooth and untroubled through the flowery vale,
O'er thy green banks once more, the wild rose blowing
Greets the young spring and scents the passing gale.
Flow, silver stream; no threatening tempest lowers,
Bright, mild, and clear by gentle waters flow,
Around thy green banks the spring's young blossoms flower,
O'er thy soft waves the balmy zephyrs flow,
Yet all in vain, for never spring's arraying
Nature in charms to thee can make it fair,
Ill fated love clouds all thy paths, portraying
Years past of bliss, and future of despair.

But in 1820 she finished her second novel, *Graham Hamilton*. This is a mere outline of a story, easy to read because well written, and without any of the phantasmagorical effects, good or bad, which make *Glenarvon* difficult. *Graham Hamilton* might, in fact, have been written by Lady Caroline had she really been only what she appeared in Miss Benger's drawing-room. Its only interest is a picture, possibly—in fact, almost certainly—inspired by her recollection of her aunt, the Duchess of Devonshire: the radiantly beautiful Lady Orville, whose eyes were so blue that they looked black at a little distance, and who so mingled thoughtless selfishness and extravagance with good nature and sensibility. The scene in which Lady Orville is called out of a splendid ball she is giving by a desperate and half-starving man, who had been ruined and imprisoned for theft on account of her refusing to discharge her debts to him, and in which she shows a really life-like mixture of horror and weakness, gives one the uncomfortable feeling that it may have been founded on fact. The circumstance of the hero's having been brought up in Scotland is a faint wraith from that seething cauldron of the past; otherwise there is nothing in the book of note: it is perhaps the least characteristic of anything she wrote. She made Colburn hold it over for two years; and she may have smoothed it down in the interval. In 1823 she was ready with her third novel, *Ada Reis*. This had been written at the instigation of Ugo Foscolo, that exiled Italian patriot who had settled on the banks of the Regent's Park Canal in Digamma Cottage; who terrified his secretary by tearing out his hair in handfuls when immersed in chess problems, and by threatening to commit suicide, at which, however, Hobhouse reassured the young man by saying, "When you have known Ugo Foscolo as long as I have, you will have as little faith in him as I have."

Foscolo had said to Lady Caroline: "Write a book that will offend nobody. Women cannot afford to shock." Here is the authentic note of the fullblown nineteenth century; but Lady Caroline, despite the ravages of distress and time, was not moulded into its pattern. When *Don Juan* reached England, a lady wrote to Murray, "Why will Lord Byron write what we may not read?" Lady Caroline said, "I cannot tell you how clever I think it is, in my heart."

Ada Reis owes something to *Vathek*, and more to the Eastern tales and to the Haidee episode of *Don Juan*; it is nevertheless complete and original in itself, and, despite the fault characteristic of the other novels —that of over-intricate plot, with its resulting lack of force—it is a very good example of its *genre*, and is distinguished by Lady Caroline's peculiar and vivid imagination. Here, as in *Glenarvon* and *Graham Hamilton*, when every credit has been given to the novelist which may be given, the paramount interest is still the autobiographical. In *Ada Reis* this element is, it is true, inferred rather than expressed, but fully obvious. The opening paragraph has a significance which could not escape anyone who had read *Manfred* or *Cain*: "According to the doctrine of Manes, there are two principles by which all things proceed, and by which all things are governed; the one is a pure and subtle essence called light, and the other is a corrupt substance called darkness. Each of these is subject to a superintending being, who has existed from all eternity. The ruler of light is supremely happy, benevolent and good; the prince of darkness is miserable himself and desirous of rendering others miserable." The character of Ada Reis, though little more than a mechanical agent in the plot, has here and there a touch one recognises; this bold and desperate being, a Georgian by birth, and of remarkable beauty, with auburn curling hair and a musical voice, had been excited by the exploits of the Corsairs and become a pirate. He took the title of Reis, or captain, from an Algerian whom he overthrew, and, after leading a life of adventure on the seas, settled in Arabia. We are not surprised to hear of his "exulting while sailing on the beautiful Mediterranean" and that he would sing with her merry followers and laugh triumphantly as his swift vessel glided amongst the islands of the Archipelago. He had murdered his mistress, the Spanish Bianca Castamela, because during his absence from her she had married another lover, and he had brought away with him the daughter she had borne him, and whom he named Fiormonda. In the Arabian desert he encountered the Jew Kabkarra, who personifies the spirit of darkness and who promised him that as the reward of his allegiance he should be a king, and his daughter the consort of an emperor. The alliance was accepted by Ada Reis, and Kabkarra presented him with a scimitar which, when drawn from its sheath, perfumed the air; in one of the many notes with which the book is supplied we are told that Damascus blades are actually so impregnated with perfume in their manufacture that the scent remains as long as the steel itself shall last. Lady Caroline had spared no pains in providing an accurate background to her phantasy, and her notes are quotations from Herrara's *History of America,* Humboldt's *Tableau de la Nature,* Tully's *Tripoli,* and *L'Europe et l'Amerique comparées.* The story goes on to describe the upbringing of Fiormonda among all the Oriental magnificence which her father, as a result of his infernal compact, could provide, and the installation of Kabkarra's mother, Shaffou Paca, as the child's governess. There is an interesting remark: "Most children think deeply if left to themselves, if leisure be allowed to the mind to expand, and a succession of lessons and trifles follow not each other too rapidly." Fiormonda was not in need of a governess, but Kabkarra's influence was all powerful, and Shaffou Paca arrived to take up the position. "She was of Egyptian origin, but her countenance was not of simple Egyptian ugliness; it seemed to exhibit a characteristic mark of every original nation. Her legs appeared to have been put together by mistake, the right one being considerably shorter and thicker than the other. She was corpulent, and her eyes, which saw even more than other eyes can see, never looked in the same direction. She had, besides, the peculiar power, like the chameleon, of fixing the one upon an object, while the other turned leisurely round, as if seeking for something else. In her voluble conversation no idea was distinct; it seemed as if an endless memory, stored with the beginnings and endings of all that ever had been, was running over the heads and hints of what she wished to express. Learning appeared to have overpowered her; she had dabbled in metaphysics until it was hardly possible to understand what she meant; she was continually misquoting passages in the dead languages." Ada Reis rashly began to speak to her on the subject of education, and was soon involved in such a stupendous oration, that 'in order to get rid of her, he sent for the child and delivered her into her hands, for it is a common practice to condemn children to the society of those with whom the parents cannot endure even for a moment to associate." Kabkarra frequently made an appearance in the palace, and always in such a manner as to produce a start of real surprise, both in the protagonists of the story and in the reader; once he was discovered in the robes of a madly dancing dervish, once as a physician; he left a reminder of himself and his influence in a present for Fiormonda consisting of a set of animated chessmen; the board was made of squares of polished ivory and jet, "the chessmen were habited in ruby and emerald suits; the dark knights were upon black steeds, richly caparisoned, their antagonists upon greys; all were formed with precision, delicacy and exquisite art—they could smile, they could use their fingers and feet, the horses pranced, the horsemen showed off their skill. The ecclesiastics moved with dignity, the castles were borne slowly forward; two were made of rose-coloured diamonds, and two of black; upon the battlements small men were discovered, busily preparing for the attack. The kings had brows which bespoke command, the queens were graceful, the pawns with plebeian rudeness appeared eager for the combat, and every piece placed itself as it started from the box, according to order." But Fiormonda received other presents. Her page, Zevahir, had been dismissed because he had been discovered talking to her without the presence of Shaffou Paca; as she one day was walking lonely in the garden, "she heard the air she had often heard played in her infancy by Zevahir; her bird flew from her and nestled in a shrub as if alarmed. She then beheld a ball, bright as a diamond, and musical as the chime of bells, rolling towards her along the smooth margin of the lake, and lightly along the bank came a youth, dressed after another fashion than that of her country, but of a countenance fair and beautiful as the day." This turned out to be Zevahir, returned to be her guardian in another form, and in reality Phaos, the representative of the spirit of light. Much as she loved him, however, he could only remain with her when she controlled her passions, and Kabkarra did everything he could to undermine the power of Phaos by giving her a girdle of jewels, the wearing of which strengthened every evil desire. Her outbreaks were frequent, and there is one short passage which has a familiar ring: "Ah, who that had seen that soft eye downcast and covered with its jetty fringe, as with a slow step she gently followed her guardians like a lamb to the altar, could possibly have believed that a moment before she had knocked down the vases in the state apartments, and had torn in pieces the celebrated veil wrought in Egypt for Bianca Castamela her mother and presented to her by Ada Reis . . . could Fiormonda, that lovely, that gentle child, have given the yellow slave that terrible bump over her right eye, or impressed a wound upon the arm of Shaffou Paca who now followed her, venting her ill-humour by ceaseless complaints?" The struggle for Fiormonda's soul continued between Kabkarra and Phaos, until, on Ada Reis's once sitting down with her to play with the chessmen, they were prevented from touching the board by the visionary appearance of both spirits, who sat down opposite each other, and began to play for the mastery of her; the diamond ball meanwhile sending out a mournful chime from the chest in which it lay. The contest ended in the victory of Kabkarra, who, telling them that the Pasha with his forces was at that moment at their gates to avenge a slight committed against him by Ada Reis, hastened them off to safety, and decided Ada Reis upon a voyage to Peru. On this voyage they encountered a profligate villain named Candulmar, who, in the absence of Phaos, gained possession of Fiormonda's heart, and in this part of the story again there are hints of past experience. "O what a dream is happiness, since it depends upon a smile or frown!" When the party had taken up their abode in Lima, Candulmar soon deserted Fiormonda for the local beauties, and, despite the numerous suitors who were attracted by her beauty and her father's wealth, she mourned his defection; this only alienated him the further, for "there is no man however unfeeling and remorseless who does not fear and dislike the reproaches of the woman he has injured." The viceroy's son, in love with Fiormonda and jealous of the influence of Candulmar, provokes the latter to a duel in which he himself is slain; the sudden appearance of Kabkarra announces an earthquake, in which the whole of Lima is laid waste, and Ada Reis, flung by the force of the convulsion into a place of safety, is guided by an Indian to the territory of a savage and degraded tribe, who make him their king, thus ironically fulfilling the promise of Kabkarra. The misery and disgust of Ada Reis at being abandoned among the subservient but vile savages are intense; one day he is sitting in his apartment when his attention is attracted by the activity of a spider. "The web grew and the insect grew; its motions were so rapid, its perseverance so great that soon it had drawn its threads from one corner of the room to the spot upon which Ada Reis stood, and now growing larger and larger, its shining eyes and grinning mouth became terrible to look upon; it spun its threads round and round Ada Reis, it moved from side to side; at length he found himself caught like a lion in its toils, and the monstrous spider stopped, staring at him in Triumph. A laugh and a yell now sounded and the word Kabkarra was pronounced. Ada Reis started backward through the silken web, then rushed forward; nothing impeded his course, not palace nor people—he found himself in a mountainous desert." The third and last volume is the account of Hades, to which Kabkarra conducted Ada Reis through an opening in the mountain-side, and where he was told that he should see his daughter as an empress. This is the part of which William Lamb, who seems to have taken a genuine interest in the book, wrote to Murray, "The incongruity of and objection to *Ada Reis* can only be got over by power of writing, beauty of sentiment, striking and effective situation etc. If Mr. Gifford thinks that there is in the first two volumes anything of excellence sufficient to overbalance the manifest faults, I still hope he will press on Lady Caroline the absolute necessity of carefully revising and reconsidering the third volume, and particularly the conclusion of the novel. Mr. Gifford I daresay will agree with me that from the time of Lucian, all the representations of the infernal regions, which have been attempted by satirical writers, such as Fielding's *Journey from this World to the Next*, have been feeble and flat. The sketch in *Ada Reis* is commonplace in its observations and altogether insufficient, and it would not now do to come with a decisive failure in an attempt of considerable boldness. I think if it was thought that anything would be done with the novel, and that the faults of its design and structure could be got over, that I could put her in the way of writing up this part a little, of giving it something of strength, spirit and novelty and of making it at once more unusual and more interesting. I wish you would communicate these my hasty suggestions to Mr. Gifford, and he will see the propriety of pressing Lady Caroline to take a little more time to this part of the novel. She will be guided by his authority, and her fault at present is to be too hasty and too impatient of the trouble of correcting and recasting what is faulty." It cannot be decided with any certainty what, if anything, William Lamb contributed of "strength, spirit and novelty" to the description of Hades; but the final incident of the book is certainly original, and perhaps he suggested it: the Hell visited by Ada Reis is, like that of *Vathek*, one of gloomy splendour and magnificent anguish, and seated at a gorgeous banquet is Fiormonda, bowed down by the weight of a diadem. There are few women in the halls of pain, as compared with the number of men, not because, as Kabkarra informed Ada Reis, women are better than men, but that "by one way or another, women are generally punished upon earth for their offences; our master receives no broken or contrite hearts here." Yet there was one present:

" 'I would converse,' said Ada Reis, 'with that thin woman; why does she weep thus? Art thou also one of these? Thy faded wreath, thy haggard air, thy lingering step declare it.'

" 'I was once one of them,' said the lady with a deep-drawn sigh, 'but I am nothing now.'

" '... What occasions you such regret?'

" 'The happy dream of life being forever past; the dread too lest I should have been wanting in gratitude and attachment to those I love so well ... my punishment is now to see the shades of everyone once dear to me pass by me with indifference; to feel intensely, but to know that none feel for me; to hear from timepieces all day and all night long, not the hours, but all my thousand follies and faults repeated, to be conscious that all my thoughts, wishes and actions are misrepresented.

Sir, can I say more? I was idolised, I am—ah, would I were only forgotten! But it is well—I lost myself. I felt the harshness and unkindness of some too keenly—I seized my pen, the pen that once knew but to write with the milk of human kindness, I dipped in gall.'

"'No woman should ever write,' said Ada Reis. The lady sighed.

"'Name to me,' said Ada Reis, 'as they pass us in long procession, these misled votaries, and tell me truly all you know of them.'

"'They have borne with me,' said the lady; 'I will never return evil for good——' As she yet spoke she mournfully turned away, and followed with the rest."

Every being in this Hell felt convinced that, given another opportunity, he or she would never sin again. The opportunity was mysteriously granted to each one, and Ada Reis saw before him the form of Bianca Castamela, his murdered mistress. In an agony of delight, he was about to clasp her in his arms, saying that they would lead another life together, when he saw her eyes fixed upon another shade—that of the man for whom she had abandoned him. In the sudden passion of rapture turned to disappointment and love to jealous rage, he seized her and plunged his knife into her bosom, thus condemning himself, as the other shades had already condemned themselves, to perpetual imprisonment. But Fiormonda had been approached by Candulmar, who came gently to her and asked for the magic flower, once given her by Phaos, which she wore in her bosom. "She looked upon him, and love, more dangerous than infectious fever, caught from his glance new fuel wherewith to consume her; she hesitated: she had forgotten his cruelty, his wickedness; she adored him, and she saw that her affection was returned." In the face of this overpowering temptation, she prayed for strength. "Scarcely had she uttered her heartfelt prayer when her spirit like a cloud dissolved and melted into air. She was borne through shrieking winds, she was carried in the lightning amongst storm and whirlwinds. Through flame and through air she saw crowding before her astonished senses all that was, is and will be—delirium never conjured up such fantastic horrors as passed before her." She was restored to earth, and, leaving behind her the ruins of Lima, she went far away to the forest of the Oronooke, where the stars are reflected in the vapour of the desert as in the bosom of a lake; where the rock-beds of the water are tinged with a black dye which has formed in the course of thousands of years, and the great river with its foaming waters seems to have burst through the thick, uninhabited woods, with their monstrous foliage and the grey, dim-eyed crocodiles. Here she lived, a hermitess, until she died, and left her history written on a scroll found in the tomb where Indians had buried her.

This book pleased Lady Caroline more than either of her other works, and it gained considerable popularity on its own merits. Lady Cowper told the bookseller to send a copy to Frederick Lamb, in case he should think it worth fifteen shillings to know what it was all about. Lady Morgan asked Murray to send it immediately; Lady Caroline, in sending the message, asked if he knew how her "prettiest song" out of *Graham Hamilton* had come to be re-published as written by Mrs. Jordan on her death-bed—Mrs. Jordan, who had made such a success of the *Country Wife*, and of whose playing of the part Leigh Hunt has left such an excellent description: "blubbering and munching bread and butter." The incident is a striking example of the opportunist and piratical methods of early nineteenth-century publishing.

With Lady Morgan she continued to correspond. The latter was writing a work on Salvator Rosa, that painter who with Claude had aroused the enthusiasm of the "Picturesque" period, which brought into English poetry and novels descriptions of autumn, and the storm-blasted mountain scenery of Byron and Mrs. Radcliffe, and into pictures those backgrounds of umber foliage and blue hills seen in the portraits of Reynolds and Gainsborough: so much so that Sir George Beaumont was wont to say that a good picture was brown, like an old fiddle, and to criticise the compositions of young painters by saying, "But where is your brown tree?"

Lady Caroline gave her useful assistance in finding out for her what Salvator Rosas were in the possession of the family. She engaged the services of William Ponsonby to the task, who to oblige his sister wrote a note to Lady Morgan with what information he already had, and a long letter to Lady Caroline on the subject, reminding her that she must herself have seen most of them. Lady Caroline wrote to Lady Morgan: "I hope you will not impute it to me that your questions are not answered; the truth is I am in the country, enjoying this most beautiful time of year, and my brother has written word that he will make all the enquiries you desire." She gives a few details of the pictures she remembers, and adds that there are two landscapes at Panshanger in "the usual dark abrupt style." But, she says. "it is not this month that I can do anything beyond staring at the flowers and trees."

While she was at Brocket, she was, she told Lady Morgan, "much annoyed by paragraphs in two papers about my turning a woman out of doors . . . it is a most shameful falsehood made by a very wicked girl, because I sent her away. She came to me as Agnes Drummond, a spinster, and ten days after hid a man in Brocket Hall. The servants in an uproar discovered him in the evening; he said first his name was Drummond, and then Fain; it was natural we should desire him to walk out, particularly as Agnes Drummond had confided to me only the day before that she had been married when only sixteen to a thief of the name of Fain; who had married her and carried away her watch and property. I trouble you with this as I see my name as having beaten her and turned her out of doors, without clothes in the night; instead of which my coachman conveyed her to an inn, and had great difficulty in making her sleep there. *She* took *my* clothes away, and seal, which were taken from her . . . her own clothes were left wet in the laundry, or they would have been sent on that night."

Lady Cloncurry was in need of a governess, and asked Lady Morgan's advice. Lady Caroline was interested in a young woman, Miss Bryan, and earnestly recommended her, but with considerable humour and common sense; she said of Miss Bryan: "She is attached to an old mathematician in Russia—a Platonic attachment—his name is Wronsky. . . . I enclose you upon trust a letter of Miss Bryan, but as there are two or three trifling mistakes of grammar, do not show it. I feel interested in her, yet she and I are not congenial souls. She is more dignified, tranquil, calm and gentle, and self-possessed than I am, and therefore if she is made to be all she can be, she will do better to bring up others. Now as everyone must and will and should fall in love it is no bad thing that she should have a happy, Platonic, remote attachment to an old mad mathematician several thousand miles off. It will keep her steady, which in truth, she is,—beyond her years. . . . She is but young, and I advise most particularly that [Lady Cloncurry] should begin as she intends to proceed. Miss Bryan is gentle, though proud, and can bear being spoken to, but she requires to be told the plain truth, whole truth, and all truth. . . .

"The power of instructing is almost a gift of nature . . . many of the best instructed are themselves very deficient in it." There was a pause in the arrangements for Miss Bryan's disposal, and then Lady Caroline took the matter up again:

"I must now tell you about Miss Bryan. She has caught cold and been very, very ill. I would not for the world have Lady Cloncurry wait for her, but if she chances to be without a proper person when well, Miss Bryan would assuredly do. However it is no loss to the girl as I feel sure she wishes to die or marry Wronsky, and therefore do nothing further about her. She is sensible, handsome, young, good, unsophisticated, independent, true, ladylike, above any deceit or meanness, romantic, very punctual about money—but she has a cold and cough, and is in love. I can't help it, can you?"

Lady Caroline had done her best for the difficult Miss Bryan; as Lady Morgan said, in showing kindness she obeyed "the instinctive impulse of a sanguine and genial disposition." A few miles away, at Panshanger, Lady Cowper was struck with admiration because her little girl offered to get up in the night to her French governess, who was ill. Lady Cowper said, "But, my love, I desire that you will not! I can't hear of mademoiselle waking you in the night!" The child very gravely replied that this was hardly fair, since, if she herself were ill, mademoiselle would certainly get up for her. Lady Cowper was filled with admiration at this understanding of "the duties of reciprocity," and no doubt the governess had every attention, but one feels that Lady Caroline would have looked after her as the most natural thing in the world, and without a thought to the duties of reciprocity.

CHAPTER TEN

She said: "Life after all that has been said of its brevity is very, very long, and more persons feel reason to complain of its slowness than of the swiftness of its course." She loved to be at Brocket, among the trees and fields of Hertfordshire; but she had lost Byron, William Lamb was no longer the husband of her youth, and she was worse than childless. She had the torments, but not the languor, of *ennui*. She told Godwin:

"I am tormented with a superabundance of activity and have so little to do, that I want you to tell me how to get on. It were all very well if one died at the end of a tragic scene, after playing a desperate part, but if one lives, and instead of growing wiser one remains the same victim of every folly and passion without the excuse of youth and inexperience, what then? . . . I have nothing to do—I mean necessarily. There is no particular reason why I should exist, it conduces to no one's happiness, and on the contrary, I stand in the way of many. Besides I seem to have lived 500 years, and feel I am neither wiser, better, nor worse than when I began . . . this is probably the case of millions but that does not mend the matter, and while a fly exists, it seeks to save itself. Forgive my writing so much about myself, and believe me, yours most sincerely,

"CAROLINE LAMB."

She tried to occupy herself with the economical management of Brocket, but the lavish habits of a lifetime were not to be re-ordered now, and all she could accomplish were short periods of rigid economy which bore hardly on the servants, accustomed to the proverbial extravagance of a large English house, and not upheld by any urge to moral regeneration which made it easy for Lady Caroline to eat next to nothing if she felt inclined. She told Lady Morgan:

"I did write a book about stables and domestic economy, upon a new and beautiful plan, but unless someone saw it and thought it good, I would not venture to publish it. Yet I wrote it while I was writing *Ada Reis*. My laundry and stables I conduct upon that plan to save myself trouble, but it is more difficult to put into practice in a home although it was done, and without success, one year. I mention this to show you that I too have been a good housewife and saved William much, but he says 'What is the use of saving in one place if you squander all away in another?' Alas, what is the use of anything? We may go on saying what is the use of anything? Till we really puzzle ourselves, as I did, as to why we exist at all."

William Lamb had perhaps reached the same enquiry, and relinquished it as unanswerable. He spent his days, apart from social diversions—for, however cynical, he was never misanthropical—reading in the library at Melbourne House or at Brocket. In a curious little memoir of him by Bulwer Lytton, printed in solid gold type on a paper of superlative gloss, a medium highly suited to the author in its sheen and glitter, though not so expressive of its subject, we find this paragraph:

"His habits were in appearance those of indolence; he went into society in the evening, he had the air of a lounger in the morning; he attended indifferently to things of small importance, and consequently he was called idle for many years of his life, decreed as idle by a vast variety of persons who were far less usefully employed than himself. During this time he read more and thought more than perhaps any person of his own station and standing." He had one interest at Brocket besides the library in his constant attention to his son. Augustus was now seventeen, tall and handsome, but hopelessly clouded in his intellect. He was put for some time in the care of a Miss Webster at Brompton, and there Lady Cowper and old Lord Melbourne went to see him. "He is a little better," said the former, "and because he is kept very quiet and almost starved, but this is the only difference. Lee says that the moment he gets the least into health they return bad again, so that he is obliged to be always pulling him down. His head was covered with the marks of leeches to-day. I mention this because Caroline's great object lately has been to persuade everybody that he was quite well, and therefore I was surprised when I heard the truth, for she had persuaded Papa and William and told me only two days ago that he was quite well now, and that she was *so happy* to find him *cured* and that he had been *10 weeks* without having a fit. I suppose she is tired of lamenting about it, so she wants to hear no more on the subject. I thought she looked foolish when I said I would go and see him, and she said, 'Don't be surprised if you find him with Leeches on his head, for it is merely done as a measure of precaution,'" The boy, said Lady Cowper, was "strong and healthy, but with the mind of a child, and always in mischief, rolling the maids about, tickling Charlotte and playing pranks, and old Nanny, when she goes out the drawing room is obliged to lock the door or else he runs down half dressed, and tumbles her on the floor and sits upon her, *n'est-ce-pas incroyable? and* this at eighteen years old. I think his fits are as bad as ever and more frequent. I went last night to the play to see *Frankenstein* and the huge creature without any sense put us all in mind of Augustus." A good deal may be said in a family letter which the writer has no idea will be published, and Lady Cowper's virtues, being of the stronger sort, did not include sensitiveness and good taste.

William Lamb did not consider Augustus's condition to be such that there was no possibility of educating him. In 1821 he engaged a young Scots doctor, Robert Lee, to be his tutor, and, in discussing his suitability for the post, he stated very clearly the qualifications he desired. "With respect to his education I must beg leave to state distinctly, that the principal object of it at present must be to teach him the Latin and Greek languages according to the mode practised in our English schools, which I shall be able to point out to him, and that he must come prepared to submit any opinion he may have formed respecting the superiority of other branches of study, or of more eligible modes of conducting this branch, to my southern propensities." Dr. Lee kept a diary of his stay at Brocket, in which he records mainly the conversation of the dinner-table. Lady Caroline was already showing, in violent outbreaks of nervous irritation, the imminence of a nervous breakdown, and he says on one occasion, "Lady Caroline talked a great deal of nonsense at dinner, but was rather more agreeable than usual, a certain prelude to a violent storm." One of the guests—for open house was still kept—was Mr. Sheridan, Sheridan's son; at a large dinner-party, "Lady Caroline thought it would be an improvement if ladies lived in houses different from their husbands, and that they only simply called upon them." If, two years later, someone had reminded her of these words, would she have believed that she had ever uttered them? "Mr. Sheridan remarked how delightful it would be to have a card left for you on the table by your husband; that before the Revolution in France, this was the case, the house was divided completely, and Mr. Lamb said it was too bad that it was all swept away . . . that there could be no doubt that it was most advisable to marry, but that those who are not rich ought not to marry at all. People who are forced to live much together, are confined to the same room, the same bed etc., are like two pigeons put under one basket, who must fight."

Harriette Wilson, and Lady Caroline's own remark—"His violence is as bad as my own"—suggest much that went on of which no actual record remains; the only direct evidence of William Lamb's behaviour shows that he exercised the serenest and most gentle tolerance, and her behaviour was by degrees becoming more exaggerated and alarming; one afternoon she was driving to pay a call, and, as she was by herself in the carriage, she preferred to ride on the box and talk to the coachman. When they drew up at the door, the footman came up to hand her down, but she called out, "I'm going to jump—you must catch me!" and sprang down into his arms; a feat which, if it seems only risky to us, would have suggested severe mental derangement to Lady Cowper; "she is such a low minded person, that is the worst of her." On another occasion, when the butler was arranging the table for a dinnerparty in the evening, Lady Caroline came in and said that the central decoration of the table wanted "feature, expression and elevation." The butler agreed, but went on laying out the plate; Lady Caroline impatiently swept the ornaments aside, and, leaping on to the table, converted herself into an épergne, expressing in her attitude the expression and elevation which she wished to see imitated. The butler instantly ran to William Lamb, who was reading in the library, and implored him to come at once. Lamb followed him into the dining-room, and "the moment he saw her, only said in the gentlest tone of expostulation, 'Caroline, Caroline!' Then took her in his arms and carried her out of doors into the sunshine, talking of some ordinary subject to divert her attention from what had happened. That evening, she received her friends with as calm a look, and tone as in happier days." With these quick outbreaks and quick recoveries it was hardly possible to alter the course of ordinary life, but it made it increasingly difficult. "The servants," said Lady Cowper, "pass through like the figures in a magic lanthorn, they come on and go off,—a new cook whom Hagard was all expectation to see from her great character and her fifty guinea wages, stayed, I believe, only one week. Dear Hagard is worth his weight in gold. These are pearls thrown to swine, such a pair of jewels as Hagard and Dawson. Hagard's philosophy talking of Caroline is so good; he says she can't be any worse, so one hopes she may get better." Another doctor was now attached to the household on what appeared to be a somewhat equivocal footing. Lady Cowper went to a concert-party at Hatfield House, where, she says, "*one* party made me sick, and that was the one from Brocket, consisting of William and Caroline and Dr. Walker; he is a friend of Lee's, always with her now. As she could make nothing of Lee, she leaves him and Augustus at Brompton, and takes this man with her into the country. It's such a low-lived thing to take a Scotch doctor for a lover, and William looks so like a fool, arriving with them and looking as pleased as Punch, and she looked so disgusting with her white cross, and a dirty gown as if she had been rolled in the kennel." The white cross was perhaps one of the diamond crosses she had had as wedding presents. It is painful to see through the medium of Lady Cowper's ungentle pen the carelessness and degeneration that came of a mind not quite itself; her dress was probably very dirty, but we need not accept the fact that she looked disgusting; nor that Dr. Walker was her lover in the ordinary sense of the term. The series of short-lived but ardent sentimental attachments she formed with young men were the chief emotional interest of her later years, and Bulwer Lytton, who was the last but one of her young friends, described them as "loves of the imagination."

But in 1824 came a reminder from the past. Byron died, and, while the world was still breathless, Medwin brought out his *Recollections of Lord Byron*. Here Lady Caroline saw for the first time exactly how he had spoken of her to other people. "She possessed an infinite vivacity, and an imagination heated by novel reading which made her fancy herself a heroine of romance, and led her into all sorts of eccentricities. She was married, but it was a match of *convenance* and no couple could be more fashionably indifferent to, or independent of, one another than she and her husband. She had never been in love, at least where the affections were concerned—and was perhaps made without a heart, as many of the sex are, but her head more than supplied the deficiency." Here, too, she saw for the first time the lines "Remember thee!" which he had written beneath her words on the title-page of *Vathek*. She had had two bad accidents while out riding: after the first, she had been "bathed, cupped and done everything to," and as soon as she could go out, she determined to ride again. The instinct was a sound one, but unfortunately the black mare threw her again, and she took to her bed once more. She was still in a low state of health when she received Medwin's book, and what she had to endure, both in the awakened recollections, the mind "visited again with memory of affliction passed" and the new anguish of seeing herself for the first time as she had been held up to the scorn of Byron's friends, and now to that of the public —all this makes it extraordinary that she could write to Medwin as collectedly as she did, and the final blow was struck when, as she was taken out in her carriage after her partial prostration, she met the funeral *cortège* of Byron on its way to Hucknall Torkard.

"*November 1824.*

"SIR,—I hope you will excuse my intruding upon your time: with the most intense interest I have just finished your book, which does you credit as to the manner in which it is executed, and after the momentary pain in part which it excites in many a bosom, will live in despite of censure—and be gratefully accepted by the public as long as Lord Byron's name is remembered—yet as you have left to one who adored him a bitter legacy, and as I feel so sure the lines 'remember thee— thou false to him, thou fiend to me—' were his—and as I have been very ill, and am not likely to trouble anyone much longer—you will, I am sure, grant me one favour—let me to you at least confide the truth of the past,—you owe it to me, you will not I know, refuse me. [She recounted to him the early days of their intimacy and Byron's giving her the carnation and the rose.] I have them still, and the woman who through many a trial has kept these relics with the romance of former ages deserves not that you should speak of her as you do. Byron never, never could say I had no heart. He never could say either that I had not loved my husband. In his letters to me he is perpetually telling me I love him the best of the two. . . . It was not vanity that visited me: I grew to love him better than virtue, Religion,—all prospects here. He broke my heart and still I love him—Witness the agony I experienced at his death and the tears your book has cost me. Yet, Sir, allow me to say that although you have unintentionally given me pain, I had rather have experienced it than not have read your book. Parts of it are beautiful, and I can vouch for the truth of much, as I read his Memoirs before Murray burnt them. Keep Lord Byron's letter to me (I have the original) and some day add a word or two to your work from his own words, not to let everyone think I am heartless . . . Indignant and miserable, I wrote *Glenarvon*. Lady B. was more angry at it than he was. From that time I put the whole as much as I could from my mind. Lord Byron never once wrote to me, and always spoke of me with contempt. I was taken ill in March this year—Mrs. Russell Hunter and a nurse—sat up with me. In the middle of the night I fancied I saw Lord Byron—I screamed, jumped out of bed, and desired them to save me from him. He looked horrible and ground his teeth at me, he did not speak; his hair was straight; he was fatter than when I knew him, and not near so handsome. I felt convinced I was to die. This dream took possession of my mind. I had not dreamed of him since we had parted. It was besides like no other dream except one of my Mother that I ever had. I am glad to think that it occurred before his death, as I never did and hope I never shall see a Ghost. I even avoided enquiring about the exact day for fear I should believe it—it made enough impression as it was. I told William and my brother and Murray at the time. Judge what my horror was, as well as grief, when, long after, the news came of his death, it was conveyed to me in two or three words—'Caroline, behave properly, I know it will shock you—Lord Byron is dead.' This letter I received when laughing at Brocket Hall. Its effect or some other cause produced a fever from which I never yet have recovered. It was also singular that the first day I could go out in an open carriage, as I was slowly driving up the hill here—Lord Byron's hearse was at that moment passing under these very walls, and rested at Welwyn. William Lamb who was riding on before me, met the procession at the turnpike, and asked whose funeral it was. He was very much affected and shocked—I of course was not told; but as I kept continually asking where and when he was to be buried, and had read in the paper it was to be in Westminster Abbey, I heard it too soon, and it made me very ill again."

In subsequent editions Medwin deleted some of the passages about her. At nearly the same time a curious attempt was made to blackmail Hobhouse. A "J. Wilmington Fleming" offered him for sale what he or she declared to be a journal of Lady Caroline Lamb; that he was able to make so plausible a forgery suggests that he must have had access to the papers of Colburn, and seen either the actual journal which Lady Caroline sent Colburn, with instructions not to publish till after her death, or the letter to Medwin which she enclosed in a letter to Colburn to be forwarded. Wilmington Fleming begins his letter, which is evidently a second application:

"I considered from passages in the paper to which I alluded—copies of which I now subjoin—that you would not wish them to become the property of a mercenary publisher, to which nothing but the extreme misery of my situation could induce me to consent." On the inside leaves of the paper, which is folded in two, he has written out the following passages which purport to be extracts from the journal:

"It is a pity that the memoranda has been destroyed, but I think a copy still exists in the possession of either Moore or Hobhouse." (This would seem to refer to the Memorials of Byron, bequeathed by him to Moore, and burned by the latter as unfit for publication.)

"Hobhouse writes that if I will give up Lord Byron's letters, to be destroyed!—he will return mine. He says that Byron should only be known to the world by his great talents and noble death, and that it is the business of a friend to draw a veil over his errors." Byron had told Murray that if he could gain possession of the letters he had written to Lady Caroline while she was in Ireland, they would make a valuable addition to his papers. Lady Caroline refused to part with them: she said, mindful of Moore, "I would not part with them—I have them now. They would only burn them and nothing of his should be burnt."

"His behaviour had changed my heart and when he informed me of —— I shuddered even at his presence."

"The first time Lord Byron said that to me *which he should not* etc."

"The first time he saw Miss Milbanke (now Lady Byron) was at *M* House and he did not like her—she was formal and stiff etc."

"The evening before the execution of Bellingham he came to me, *pale* and exceedingly agitated, and said he must see him die; he was silent and restless and I liked him less on that evening; he departed early; and appeared at breakfast the next morning, calm and tranquil. I have seen him suffer, he said, and he made *no confession*."

"It was *me*, and no General that introduced Lord Byron to the King. It was not etc."

"He used to lament the mischief he had occasioned, saying he and W—— L—— were like Hamlet's two pictures, etc."

"It has been reported that I visited Lord Byron's lodgings in the guise of a page. Johnny Greene was my page at that time."

This document is in the Manuscript Department of the British Museum; its origin remains obscure, as that other rumour mentioned by Byron that a certain lady was approached by an agent of Lady Caroline's and told that her name would be inserted in *Glenarvon* unless she paid £500, which the said lady agreed to do. This story is unlikely, among Lady Caroline's many faults, rapacity was not one; and the sensation caused by the publishing of such a *roman à clef* was the very forcing-house for such stories.

But the subject of them was now oblivious of everything but her own domestic tragedy. Her attacks of wildness, in which she smashed crockery, and once the doctor's watch, had at long last determined William Lamb that he would no longer live with her; she who had lightly proclaimed that it would be a much better arrangement if ladies and their husbands lived in separate establishments was now to realise the anguish of being turned out of her husband's house. That she could not be left in the position of the mistress of Brocket was obvious; but someone—it is better not to guess who—had the inexcusable cruelty to let her hear herself talked of as insane. The word drove her into further paroxysms, and when, one evening, William Lamb left Melbourne House in fury, and drove down to Brocket, where he settled himself in his room, as he imagined alone, he heard a noise outside the door, and, opening it, found her on the floor in convulsions of grief, having followed him all the way into Hertfordshire.

But the decision, so slowly reached, was irrevocable, and the whole family could now exert themselves in trying to make her consent to a separation. She wrote a letter—we do not know to whom, for the name has been erased:

"DEAR ——,—Ask of those you think great scholars whether the meaning of the word 'amicable' separation after twenty years of mutual attachment, resentment, forbearance, agreements to part, making it up again—but no, I will explain it. It is to idolize and flatter, to be entirely governed by a woman who every day errs and is never restrained nor reproved while she is young, in health and accounted clever— it is to retain her by protestations of kindness and love when others wished to take her away—it is to laugh, show benignant humour, independent ideas, proud spirit and when perhaps by her own fault she becomes miserable, ill and lonely, to find out all her errors—blaze them to the world and have straight waistcoats, physicians, with all the aristocracy of the country to say she had better go—go where? Will you but tell me that, only do not as Frederick Lamb, Lady Cowper and others would say, answer to the D——l,—let them go there if they like it; I will not if I can help it. Excuse me for troubling you; pray mark that in this truly *amicable* arrangement I am accused of being *passionate* (when ill-used)—did they never find that out before? I, however, still love the hand upraised to shed my blood."

The arrangements went on, not without the intervention of William Ponsonby, who, Lady Cowper said, "Wrote William such an impertinent letter that the latter says he will have no communication with him—which letter was a great advantage to us, as it steadied our brother and put the other in the wrong. These are the things he says in his letter to William. That by this marriage William got a brilliant connection which his family *wanted* (was there ever such an ass?) and that he never would allow his sister to be trampled upon by him or his family, (as if our forbearance was not proverbial)." William Ponsonby may have been tactless when he urged the social advantages to the Lambs of the marriage with his sister, but, so far as actual fact went, he was undoubtedly quite right, however unpalatable it might be to Lady Cowper. At first the latter was anxious about the affair, as "William was foolish and used to go and see her and listen to her stories, and laugh—but then came the quarrels, and she misrepresented him and told William Ponsonby of his beating her, which was not true and he and our William quarrelled, upon which the latter took the wise determination of seeing her no more, and wrote her word so." Two referees were arranged, Lord Cowper for William Lamb, and the Duke of Devonshire for Lady Caroline. It was a melancholy office for Hart to have to perform by her; Lady Caroline seemed tolerably resigned, and Lady Cowper took the credit of this to herself. "In a quiet way I have bullied the bully—she threatened and raged for the first half hour I was with her, about the book and letters etc. [this perhaps refers to a threat that she herself would publish her journal] and when she had done, I said in the quietest way, 'Well I see all accommodation is impossible,' for this is exactly what William said to me last night—he said it was only trifling to try a private arrangement and that now he had quite made up his mind to go into court, that many things might be said disagreeable on both sides, but that this in his opinion was a trifle compared with the advantage of having everything finally and completely settled, and so I went on saying, I was not quite of that opinion, but that as she and William had both made up their minds, there was no help for it.

"This produced a violent abusive letter to him next morning, which he did not understand till I explained it, and next morning came a letter from her to Lord Cowper, begging of him to speak to the Duke of Devonshire, and saying how anxious she was for *any* settlement which would keep them out of court—as there was no use in their appearing in court like Mr. & Mrs. Bang reviling each other, and so Lord Cowper is to meet the Duke, and I hope it will all be settled. I think the arrangement will be £2,500 now, and £3,000 on Papa's death, a great deal more than she deserves—but I think it very well worth while to get rid of her, and to have the whole thing settled quietly."

Nothing perhaps shows the change which years had made on Lady Caroline more than this shrinking from the public gaze of which she would once have been oblivious. The proceedings continued, but not with sufficient rapidity and decision for Lady Cowper, who thought Lady Caroline should be dislodged, and said of William Lamb:

"He wants energy so much, and somebody at his back to push him on. In his own determination of parting, I see no wavering, but he does not know what to do, and instead of taking a House for her *coute qu'il coute* and ordering her into it, he hesitates and thinks of the price, and fancies she will go abroad or to Melbourne, whereas it seems clear to me that she had no intention of the sort, and only talks of these plans to gain time." William Lamb still could not keep away, and Lady Cowper was naturally uneasy at the possibility, remote as it was, of his decisions being subverted.

"William is returned to town—I have not seen him; but I fancy he goes to *see* her too much, which I think foolish, (tho' I do not doubt his steadiness) but she is sure to take advantage of everything—however as she sent Papa word that she would be out of the house by August 1st, I think she must keep to that, and William is to take a house for her before that time."

Lady Caroline, though struggling faintly to recover herself and behave calmly, gave way to frequent fits of despair, not the least bitter cause of which was leaving Brocket Hall, the grounds of which she had so ardently loved, and which now seemed like the Paradise of evicted Adam. She wrote to Lady Morgan:

"I am afraid you have seen me under great irritation, and under circumstances that might try anybody. I am too miserable. You have not yet advised me what to do—I know not, care not. O God, it is a punishment severe enough. I can never recover it. It is fair to William Lamb to mention that since I saw you, he has written a kinder letter, but if I am sent to live by myself, let them dread the violence of my despair—better far go away. Every tree, every flower, will awaken bitter reflections. . . . I cannot bear it. I would give all I possessed on earth to be again what I once was. I would now be obedient and gentle, but I shall die of grief. . . . My life has not been the best possible. The slave of impulse—I have rushed forward to my own destruction."

The following, which is perhaps one of her two best poems, she wrote in the park while she was waiting to go. It was a keener edge on her anguish that this month was the anniversary of her wedding, and the servants and villagers had, as usual, celebrated it with a feast. Hagard, who had been described as being, in Lady Caroline's service, a pearl thrown to swine, had been moved by the occasion and wept at the prospect of her banishment. The Welwyn band, which had so often enlivened her fêtes or merely added to the charm of the park by playing their airs under her encouragement, who had assisted at her strange rites when she burned the symbols of her fatal passion, had now gathered for the last time, and played as heartily as ever.

> Little birds in yonder grove,
> Making nests and making love,
> Come, sing upon your favourite tree
> Once more your sweetest songs to me.
> An exile from these scenes I go,
> Whither I neither care nor know;
> Perhaps to some far distant shore,
> Never again to hear you more.
> The river Lea glides smoothly by,
> Unconscious of my agony.
> This bursting sigh, this last sad tear
> On quitting all I hold so dear,
> Are felt, are heard, are seen by none,
> Left as I am by everyone. . . .

144

Where'er I go, God bless you all,
And thus I leave thee, Brocket Hall.
Time was a youthful, happy child,
Thoughtless, undaunted, gay and wild,
I came from home and parents dear
To find a home and husband here.
My joyous days with youth are fled,
My friends are either changed or dead,
My faults, my follies, leave alone,
They live in the mouth of everyone,
And still remain when all is gone.
This is my twentieth marriage year,
They celebrate with Hagard's cheer,
They dance, they sing, they bless the day
I weep the while—and well I may
Husband nor child to greet me come,
Without a friend, without a home,
I sit beneath my favourite tree;
Sing, then, my little birds to me,
In music, love, and liberty.

William Lamb had taken a small house for her in town, and she was there for a short time, meditating going to Paris. Now that the separation was concluded, an appearance of perfect amity was maintained by the Lambs. She wrote to Lady Morgan, asking her to call.

"I have permission to see all my friends here, and this is not William's house; besides he said he wished me to see everyone, and Lady —— called, and asked me whom I wished to see. I shall therefore shake hands with the whole Court Guide before I go. The only question I want you to solve for me is, shall I go abroad? Shall I throw myself upon those who no longer want me, or shall I live a good sort of a half kind of life, in some cheap street, a little way off the City Road, Shoreditch, Camberwell or upon the top of a shop, or shall I give lectures to little children, and keep a seminary, and thus earn my bread? Or shall I write a kind of quiet everyday novel full of wholesome truths, or shall I attempt to be poetical, or beg my friends for a guinea a piece and their names, publish my work upon the best foolscap paper, or shall I fret, fret, fret and die, or shall I be dignified and fancy myself as Richard II did when he picked up the nettle upon a thorn? . . .

"They have broken my heart but not my spirit and if I will but sign a paper, all my rich relations will protect me, and I shall no doubt go with an Almack ticket to heaven."

She decided to go to Paris, and set off with one maid on August 12th, 1824. Lady Cowper said, "Conceive what luck! She marched out without beat of drum last Friday morning, at 8 o'clock by the steam boat to Calais, so that I think there is little fear of her wheeling back now. She will, I trust, have been so sick as to feel little anxiety to cross the water again directly. Otherwise I should have expected to see her back next day. Lady Granville [Leveson-Gower] is very kind to have facilitated her going instead of trying to stop it, as almost all selfish people would have done under such circumstances. The rooms are now locked up safely, so I think there is no fear of her making a lodgment there again (even if she wished it). She went off in better temper and in a better frame of mind than I have seen her for a great while, and she behaved remarkably well when I took her down the last night, before she went, to wish Papa goodbye—she was very quiet and said nothing. William is *aux anges*, as happy as possible."

But she did not perch long in her uneasy, aimless flight, and a few months later she returned to England, where on landing she communicated with Lady Morgan:

"My situation in life now is new and strange; I seem to be left to my own fate most completely and to take my chance, rough or smooth, without the smallest interest being expressed in me. It is for good purposes no doubt, besides I must submit to my fate, it being without remedy. I am now with my maid at the Ship Tavern, Water Lane, having come over from Calais—I have no servants, pages, carriage, horses nor fine rooms—the melancholy of my situation in this little dingy apartment is aroused by the very loud jovial laughter of my neighbours who are smoking in the next room."

What was to happen next? We do not know the means by which it was achieved but she ultimately returned to Brocket. It must have been a struggle, and Lady Caroline was probably correct when she inferred that William Lamb was willing enough to let her return, and that the plan was opposed by his relations. She wrote the following lines:

You ask my wish—the boon I crave,
O grant it—leave me what I have.
Leave me to rest upon my bed
With broken heart, with weary head.
No stormy passions now arise,
Nor tears relieve these suffering eyes;
No age no love, disturb me now,
To God's avenging power I bow.
You've yielded to a wicked crew,
Who ruin me, who laugh at you;
Sweep out the gore, and while you can
Think for yourself, and be a man!

William Ponsonby—"my brother William my kind guardian angel"—
was at hand to look after her, and perhaps on this occasion his intervention was more diplomatic. At all events, she returned to Brocket;
Lady Cowper said, "We have not dared to tell Papa of her being there
at all," but William Lamb removed from there himself. He would
do anything for her except live with her; he wrote to her continually,
and often rode down to see her, and people in general did not realise
that the arrangement was anything but the fashionable appearance
of a separation.

In spite of everything that had passed, she was still fascinating, and
at the age of forty she made the third of her considerable conquests.

Some ten years previously, while driving out in her carriage, she
had come across an old man who had met with an accident, and, instantly stopping and alighting, she had him taken up and conveyed to
Brocket. The incident had reached the ear of young Bulwer Lytton
at Knebworth House, who had been inspired by it to write some
verses, which he sent to Lady Caroline; the latter was pleased with
them, and asked him to come and see her. It was not his first visit to
Brocket, for his parents had taken him there when he was a child, and
Lady Caroline had drawn his portrait as "Seul sur la terre"; the
acquaintance was renewed, and by 1825, when Lytton was an under-
graduate at Cambridge, he was passing through a brief but uncomfortable stage of adoration. He has left a description of her as she appeared
at this time; he says she "looked much younger than she was, thanks
perhaps to a slight, rounded figure, and a childish mode of wearing her

hair, which was of a pale golden colour, in close curls." He was not surprised when she showed him a letter of Byron's, in which the latter had said, "You are the only woman I know who never bored me"; her conversation, he said, was exquisitely interesting, with its rapid changes from profound sentiment to childish nonsense, and all delivered in her soft and lisping voice. Her conversation about Byron had no "littleness." "Whatever faults she found in his character, she fired up if any one else abused him." He spent days beside her, in the most entrancing intimacy, always expecting that the next day would produce a yet more poignant happiness; he did not doubt that she loved him. He said, "When she thought herself dying she sent for me, and there was nothing theatrical in this; the doctors told me there was everything to apprehend. I sat by her bedside for hours. When I left she wrote me a few words, though expressly forbidden by the doctors to do so."

When he returned, however, for another visit, it was Christmas, and a large party was preparing to drive over to Lady Cowper's ball at Panshanger, Lytton expected to go in Lady Caroline's carriage, but that seat was taken by young Russell, an illegitimate son of the Duke of Bedford, who was also very much at home at Brocket.

To crown his suspicion, jealousy, and grief, Lytton saw that Russell was wearing the famous ring once given by Byron to Lady Caroline, and only worn by those she loved. Lytton had worn it several times himself, and had refused to accept it as a present, on the ground of its great sentimental value. When the party returned late from the ball, he said coldly to Lady Caroline that he would say good-bye, as he would be gone the next morning before she was up. Early next morning, however, a note was brought to his room asking him not to go without seeing her. "She entreated me to forgive her, threw her arms about me and cried. Of course she persuaded me to stay. We rode out. Russell went with us. Although she certainly did not try to make me jealous, I soon perceived that she felt for him that love of the imagination she had felt before for me. She could not help liking me in an affectionate way but he was the idol of the moment. I was miserable." Things became worse and worse, so much so that after dinner, when music was going on in the drawing-room, Lytton lay on the sofa, his eyes suffused with tears. Lady Caroline behaved very badly; she saw him, and said out loud: "Don't play this melancholy air. It affects Mr.

Bulwer so that he is actually weeping." This piece of heartlessness successfully dissipated the young man's illusions, but it is much to his credit that, when the first burst of anger and disappointment was over, he felt, and continued to feel, admiration and affection as a friend.

He dashed off some of his emotion in the fragment of a novel, *De Lyndsay*, almost purely autobiographical, and therefore containing another portrait of Lady Caroline which one is glad to add to the gallery. "Lady Melton was less beautiful than any of his previous loves, but her large, languishing eye, a lip which eloquently aided the magic of her glance, an exceedingly musical voice and a form in whose delicate and fairy-like proportions a Phidias could have found no fault, invested her with a pervading and indefinable charm, far more attractive to Rupert than the inanimate perfection of Lady Stanway, or the sensual luxuriance of Mrs. Danvers Mountjoy."

He also addressed some further verses to her:

> *The world that mingles smiles with blows*
> *Thy worth but poorly prized,*
> *For love is wine, and softens shame,*
> *Where both are undisguised.*
> *But all thy woes have sprung from feeling,*
> *Thine only guilt was not concealing.*

This poem made an impression on another admirer of Lady Caroline, Rosina Doyle Wheeler, the beautiful bad-tempered creature who became Lytton's wife. One of the few manifestations of agreeable feeling which she made in the course of her unfortunate life was her sincere and youthful attachment to Lady Caroline Lamb. The connection was not at all approved of; Miss Lætitia Landon, though only seventeen at the time, wrote a "remarkably sensible" letter dissuading Rosina from the intimacy; "rouging her face and being intimate with Lady Caroline Lamb" were two of the charges brought against her by old Mrs. Bulwer, anxious with but too much reason, as it afterwards turned out, to prevent a match between Rosina and her son. But Lytton praised and commended her taste, and she replied in a letter, "I do not deserve all the praises bestowed on me by Mr. Bulwer . . . my love for Lady Caroline is nothing but selfishness. What is called propriety (but which

149

is often nothing more than the would-be mask of heartlessness), long made me refuse to know her. It was by an accident that I became acquainted with her. To be so and to love her are one."

But the figures pass as in a dream. "How can I write?" she answered a suggestion of Lytton's. "Even imagination must have some materials on which to work. I have none. Passions might produce sentiment of some sort, but mine are all calmed or extinct.

"Memory—a waste with nothing in it worth recording. Happy, healthy, contented, quiet, I get up at half past four, ride about with Hagard and see harvestmen at work in the pretty, confined green country; read a few old books, see no one, hear from no one . . . this contrast to my sometime hurried life delights me. Besides, I am well, and that is a real blessing to oneself and one's companions. When you were so kind to me, how ill, how miserable I was. . . . What are you writing now, May I not be allowed to know?

"Farewell, give my adoration to the dear sea, whose every change I worship, and whose blue waves I long to dip in, provided two old women take me out again safely. . . . To-morrow William Lamb says he will come. He has been at Hastings, with which he was delighted as far as scenery goes, and climate. But he felt dull, knowing no one there, and having nothing to do. Without wife or parliament, or trouble of any kind, he ought now to have found in perfect quiet the true enjoyment he pined for. Yet if I mistake not, he is less happy than when plagued with these apendages. If there are two p's in that word, imagine one and pray excuse my spelling."

The long days of quiet, seeing no one, hearing from no one, riding about the fields to watch the harvesters, or sitting indoors, reading old books, had built up again the fragile structure of her mind. Books, music, the green shades of Brocket park, these pleasures, "Like the last taste of sweets, were sweetest last." She dwelt more and more on her husband, as her imagination slowly withdrew itself, healed from the horrible passion that, like the shirt of Nessus, had wrapped her in a sheet of flame. She told Lady Morgan in one of the last letters she wrote:

"I never can love anything better than what I thus tell you. William Lamb first, my mother second, Byron third, my boy fourth, my brother William fifth . . . last my *petit* friend Russell, because he is my aunt's

150

godson, because when he was three I nursed him, because he had a hard-to-win, free and kind heart, but chiefly because he stood by me when no one else did."

"That dear, that angel, that misguided and misguiding Byron, whom I adore, although he left that dreadful legacy on me, my memory"— she could now think of him without agony, but merely with the un-utterable solemnity that is conferred on any great experience by the past. Her living feelings had once more returned to their first object, and she wrote her best poem to William Lamb:

> Loved one, no tear is in my eye,
> Though pangs my bosom thrill,
> For I have learned when others sigh
> To suffer and be still.
> Passion and Pride and Flattery strove,
> They made a wreck of me,
> But O, I never ceased to love,
> I never loved but thee.
>
> My heart is with our early dreams,
> And still thy influence knows,
> Still seeks thy shadow on the stream
> Of memory as it flows;
> Still hangs o'er all the records bright
> Of moments brighter still,
> Ere love withdrew his starry light,
> Ere thou hadst suffered ill.
>
> 'Tis vain, 'tis vain; no human will
> Can bid that time return,
> There's not a light on earth can fill
> Again love's darkened urn.
> 'Tis vain, upon my heart, my brow,
> Broods grief no words can tell,
> But grief itself were idle now—
> Loved one, fare thee well.

William Lamb was now, however, recalled to an active life. Canning, upon his return as Prime Minister, made him Chief Secretary for Ireland, and he went over, leaving Caroline and Augustus at Brocket. She wrote to him, asking him to go and see Lord Duncannon if he found himself in the neighbourhood, and added:

"I am sure you will be glad to hear that Frederick Lamb came over with Emily to see me, and sat with me an hour. . . . He does not look at all well, and wears long, bushy hair, which I think makes him look thinner, but it is not, as ours is, turning grey."

And now in December she began to show signs of an illness very different from the nervous attacks which, as much as the colds and low fevers, had kept her in bed so often before: a disease, the very last which should have attacked the fairy-like form, the delicate Ariel, the little Faerie Queene; however much she might be thought to have brought her troubles on herself, she had had, in her encounter with Byron's funeral, one stroke of malignant fate; and now she sustained another: she was attacked by dropsy. The horrors, the discomforts and disfigurement of this disease, which she might have borne so ill, and thus reduced herself once more to complete distraction, she nevertheless endured with absolute fortitude; her behaviour in this illness seems to establish her right to respect in her other sufferings: as if, in spite of so much wretchedness of a sort that we can understand, she felt that she had known pain, and that this was nothing. Dr. Goddard wrote to Lamb giving him particulars of the symptoms, and, as she felt too ill to write, he also wrote a letter to him at her dictation:

"I really feel better; the medicine agrees with me and I have everything I can possibly want. . . . Augustus has not been well, perhaps he leads too regular a life, and does not take enough exercise and too much tea and bread and butter. Everybody I have seen makes great enquiry after you and after him. . . . I take my simple medicines, and as Dr. Goddard is writing for me, he will probably tell you what they are, (blue pills, squills, and sweet spirits of nitre, with an infusion of Cascarilla bark). God bless you, my dearest William. I will write to you myself very soon; do not forget to write a line to me. Everything at Brocket is doing quite well."

She was brought to Melbourne House in order to be in London for special advice, but in January she felt, and it was clear, that she must die. She asked for William Lamb, but the slowness of communication, and his failure to understand at first how serious the situation was, prevented his coming immediately; when he did arrive, she did not, as she would once have done, reproach him for his neglect. Although so much had altered them to the eyes of other people, they were then to each other what they had been in their youth. There is no account of their last meeting; but William Ponsonby, all animosity forgotten, said afterwards, "William Lamb behaved as I always knew he would."

He was not in the room when she died, but Caroline George "had hold of her hand," and she died "without any pain, and from complete exhaustion."

Lady Cowper said "he was hurt at the time, and rather low next day, but he is now just as usual, and his mind filled with Politics." It was not true; and years afterwards, when Augustus was dead and the last relic of his marriage disappeared, he would say moodily, "Shall I meet her in another world?"

To find her one must return to the scraps and fragments, so nugatory in themselves, but all instinct with that strange vitality that emanated from her to everything she touched. The last contribution is the obituary notice which appeared in the *London Gazette* for February 1828. It has been ascribed to William Lamb. It touched on her connection with Byron. "The world is very lenient to the mistresses of poets, and perhaps not without justice, for their attachments have something of excuse; not only in their object but in their origin, they arise from imagination, not depravity. . . .

"There are many yet living who drew from the opening years of this gifted and warm-hearted being hopes which her maturity was not fated to realise. To them it will be some consolation to reflect that her end was what the best of us might envy, and the harshest of us approve."

She was buried in Hatfield Church, in the country she loved so much.

Lie lightly on her, gentle earth!

BIBLIOGRAPHY

Airlie, Lady: *Lady Palmerston and her Times, In Whig Society*
Annual Biography and Obituary, 1829
Boehm, Ulrich von: *Modes and Manners of the 19th Century*
Bentley's Miscellany
Berry, Miss: *Journal*
Byron: *Correspondence with Lady Melbourne*
Dyce, A.: *Table Talk of Samuel Rogers*
Dunckley, Henry: *Life of Lord Melbourne*
Dallas, R. C.: *Recollections of Lord Byron*
Foster, V.: *The Two Duchesses*
Galt, John: *Byron*
Granville, Countess of: *Private Correspondence of Earl Gower*
Gower, H. Leveson: *Letters of Harriet Countess of Granville*
Gleg, G. R.: *Personal Reminiscences of the Duke of Wellington*
Gardiner, M.: *Conversations of Byron with Lady Blessington*
Hayward, A.: *Sketches of Eminent Statesmen*
Harness, W.: *The Life of Mary Russell Mitford*
Hobhouse, J. C.: *Recollections of a Long Life*
Holland, Lady: *Journal*
Hall, S. C.: *Memories of Great Men and Women of the Age*
Kemble, Fanny: *Recollections of a Girlhood*
La Belle Assemblée
Lamb, Lady Caroline: *Glenarvon, Graham Hamilton, Ada Reis, Fugitive Pieces*
Lockhart, J. A.: *Memoirs of the Life of Scott*
Literary Gazette, 1828
Lytton, Bulwer: *Life and Literary Remains, Memoir of Lord Melbourne*
Love at Head Quarters
Lee, Dr. R.: *Extracts from the Diary of Dr. Robert Lee*
Mayne, Ethel Colburne: *Byron*
Morgan, Lady: *Memoirs of Lady Morgan, The Book of the Boudoir, Passages in My Autobiography*
Mitford, John: *The Private Life of Lord Byron,* comprising his Voluptuous Amours
Medwin, T.: *Conversations with Lord Byron*
Moore, T.: *Letters and Journals of Lord Byron*
Mundy, Harriot: *The Journals of Mary Frampton*
Newman, Bertram: *Life of Lord Melbourne*
Notes and Queries, v. 10
Ponsonby, Sir John: *The Ponsonby Family*
Paul, Charles Kegan: *William Godwin and his Contemporaries*
Rabbe, Felix: *Les Maitresses Authentiques de Lord Byron*
Redding, Cyrus: *Fifty Years of Recollections*
Sanders, Lloyd: *The Holland House Circle, Lord Melbourne's Papers*
Sichel, Walter: *Sheridan*
Simpson, James: *Paris after Waterloo*
Smiles, Samuel: *A Publisher and his Friends*
Torrens, Mac Cullagh: *Memoirs of Lord Melbourne*
Temple Bar, v. 53
Wharton, Grace: *Queens of Society*
Wilson, Harriette: *Memoirs of Herself*
Wyndham, Mrs. Hugh: *Correspondence of Lady Sarah Spencer*

INDEX